HOW TO DRIVE A CAR

A Complete Guide and Handbook to the Subtleties of Motoring under Present Day Road Traffic Conditions.

AMBERLEY

Originally published in 1933.
This edition published 2014

Amberley Publishing
The Hill, Stroud
Gloucestershire, GL5 4EP

www.amberley-books.com

British Library Cataloguing in Publication Data.
A catalogue record for this book is available from the British Library.

ISBN 978 1 4456 3579 8
EBOOK ISBN 978 1 4456 3596 5

Typesetting and Origination by Amberley Publishing.
Printed in the UK.

LIST OF CHAPTERS

"If there were a better oil than Wakefield Castrol I should use it"

HOLDER of the WORLD'S LAND SPEED RECORD OF 272 m.p.h.

How to Drive a Car

CHAPTER I.

How a Car is Controlled. What to Know Before Venturing on the Road. Starting and Stopping a Car.

The wide, open road, stretching away into the blue distance, the soft breath of the wind on your face, the faint hum of the car, the scents of the countryside, and *your* hands on the wheel. Is that your dream? Is that the wish that will come true in a few short weeks, when you take delivery of your new car and venture for the first time on the King's highway?

If it is, then this little book will be of value through all the stages of your novitiate, from the moment when you first feel the lean, firm rim of the steering wheel between your gloved hands, and are thrilled—gloriously thrilled—as you find how great is the power you so easily master, right up to the time when, with serene confidence, you can take the wheel of *any* car and drive it as if you had handled it all your life.

There is comparatively little to be learned before you can take a car on the road. On the other hand, there is much that you should "pick up" as your hours at the wheel speed by—all the big and little refinements of handling a car in a really capable, understanding manner. These things are learned easily by some drivers, while others, even after years on the road, never handle a car really expertly, because they have never taken the trouble to grasp the requirements which are all pointed out in the ensuing pages in order to assist your observation and make the delightful art of car driving more readily understood.

Driving Tuition.

Although many people learn to drive under the tuition of a friend or relative, this is not always the best course to pursue. The mere fact that the tutor and pupil are well known to one another often prevents the former from being as firm and frank in his comments as is really desirable. Furthermore, the expert driver does not always make the best teacher.

For these reasons it is an excellent plan to obtain driving lessons from a reputable motoring school where the staff is specially trained in the best methods of teaching beginners. Furthermore, special models and diagrams are usually available at such a school by means of which an elementary knowledge of the mechanism can be picked up far more readily than by verbal explanations. Most people find that such knowledge is of great assistance in gaining confidence at the wheel.

Nervousness Banished by Interest.

The first drive is far too wonderful to be spoiled by fear or nervousness; besides, there is an altogether special interest in learning the different manœuvres—how to steer, to stop and restart, to reverse—which drives timidity away. But to be taken straight out on to the road without having been, as it were, allowed to "make friends" with a car—to learn a little about it—would obviously be foolish and unpractical. Whether one is going to be taught to drive by a friend or going to attend one of the recognized schools of motoring, it is important to make oneself familiar at the very start with the controls of a car, which are more similar on the different makes than they may appear to be at first sight. Practically all cars nowadays have the same controls.

2

HOW TO DRIVE A CAR.

The Controls Explained.

First, there is the steering hand wheel; then, at the foot of the column to which this is attached, are two large pedals. That on the left is invariably used for operating the clutch, while the right-hand one applies the brakes. There is a third pedal, much smaller than the others, which is found either between the clutch and brake pedals or on the extreme right. This small control is known as the accelerator pedal, and pressing on it causes the car to go faster, because it controls the power developed by the engine. For the moment, the hand-brake lever and gear control need not be considered.

Purpose of the Clutch.

The clutch is a device which connects the engine to the gearbox so that the power is ultimately delivered to the road wheels. When the pedal is up, the clutch is said to be "in," and if the car is in gear it will move along, provided that the engine is running. Pressing the pedal down puts the clutch "out," which means that, however fast or slowly the engine is running, it will not have an effect on the running or otherwise of the car. The clutch pedal is, so to speak, used to switch power off the wheels without stopping the engine. The learner is often confused by these terms "in" and "out," which refer to the hidden parts of the clutch; remember, then, that to put the clutch "out," disconnecting the engine, you press the pedal *down*.

The brake pedal, as its name implies, slows down the car, or will bring it to a standstill, according to how hard it is applied. The accelerator pedal is so set that when the car is stationary and the pedal is left alone the engine will receive just enough "mixture" (petrol and air) to turn round slowly; it is then said to be "idling." The farther this pedal is depressed the faster the engine will go. A spring brings this pedal back to normal position, so that the engine will slow down immediately the foot is removed. Generally speaking, a very light touch is required for the accelerator pedal.

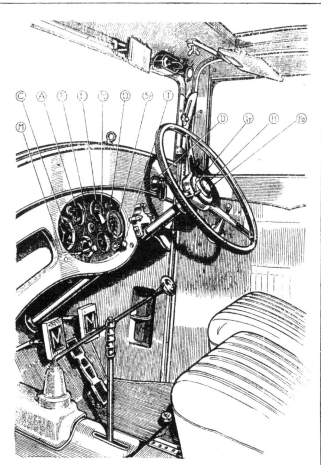

A typical layout for the instruments and controls of a popular car (Morris). The rectangular pedals operate the clutch and brakes and there is a central organ-type pedal to control the throttle. The gear lever and hand brake are operated with the left hand. The parts indicated by lettering are: A, ammeter; C, clock; D, direction signal switch; H, horn button; Hd, dip-switch headlamp control; Is, ignition switch; It, ignition timing lever; L, lighting switch; M, mixture control; O, oil pressure gauge; P, petrol gauge; Sp, speedometer; T, hand throttle.

HOW TO DRIVE A CAR.

Only Two Pedals Used at a Time.

Lest the fact that there are three pedals, while you have only two feet, should alarm you, it is as well to understand from the beginning that a case never, in any emergency, occurs when you have to press down more than two pedals at a time. The left foot is used to operate the clutch pedal and the right foot operates either the accelerator or the brakes.

Turning the steering wheel when the car is stationary will convey nothing to the beginner, as turning the wheel when the vehicle is moving is usually quite easy, while it is difficult—not to say almost impossible on some vehicles—to turn it if the car is standing still.

Why the Hand Brake Stays "On."

You will notice that the hand brake, if pulled back in the ordinary way, stays where it is put ; there is a catch, released either by an additional handle which must be grasped with the ordinary lever, or a trigger which must be pulled up ; this lifts the catch, which is forced by a spring in between the teeth on the quadrant in which the lever moves. The object of this ratchet is to keep the brake "on" if the car is left standing, particularly on a hill. When it is desired to release the brake, the lever must first be pulled "on" a little farther before the catch can be freed.

As regards the gear control, this may be of two types, one of which (not now popular) is equipped with a "gate," consisting of four or five small recesses into which the lever may be placed ; while the other, known as the ball-and-socket type, consists of a lever, growing, as it were, out of a hemisphere, which can be pushed into positions corresponding to those in the gate, but invisible. This, at first sight, may seem a little complicated, but one soon learns the position of the gears with a little practice.

However, gear changing comes later on in the process of learning to drive, and the manipulation of the lever will be described in more detail later. Let it suffice that the object of the gearbox is to make the work of the engine easier when starting away from a standstill or climbing a steep hill, and for allowing the car to be driven backwards when required, while keeping the engine running in the same way as normally.

Before leaving the gearbox, however, we must answer a question which the reader will probably be asking if he has fully grasped our description of the controls. The question is: "Why can a car be left stationary with the engine running and no one in it to depressed the clutch pedal, as in such circumstances the clutch is 'in,' and is, therefore, connecting the engine to the gearbox?" The answer is that there is another means of disconnection in addition to the clutch, which is brought into action when the gear lever is placed in a central position, called "neutral."

As we shall describe later, there is a break in the transmission when the gear lever is in neutral which prevents the engine from driving the car, although the clutch is "in." If the gear lever is placed in any other position, however, the engine will drive the rear wheels unless the pedal is held down to put the clutch "out" and so effect a disconnection.

The Throttle and Ignition Levers.

It is not intended, nor is it necessary, in this book to deal with the "why and wherefore" of the engine, carburetter and ignition system, whether the latter be the widely used coil and battery system or the alternative magneto. Readers will find these matters dealt with fully in "The Motor Manual" and the "Motor Electrical Manual" (Temple Press publications), which are practically indispensable to every motorist. Reference must, however, be made to the ignition and throttle controls or levers. Neither are actually essential fitments, but on a number of cars they are part of the control. The throttle lever, like the accelerator pedal, regulates the amount of explosive mixture with which the engine is supplied, and is usually interconnected to the same throttle valve; either hand or foot can, therefore, be used to regulate the power delivered by the engine, but only the foot is employed in the ordinary course of driving. The hand control is used to set the position of the throttle so that when the accelerator pedal is released the engine will not actually stop, but will continue to run slowly, proportionately to the setting of the hand-

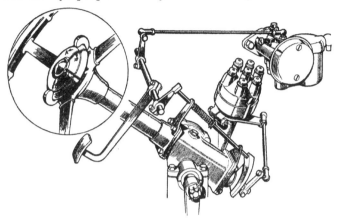

A drawing which shows a common arrangement for connecting hand levers with the throttle and the ignition distributor. The throttle is also operated by the accelerator pedal.

throttle lever. On cars with only an accelerator pedal and no hand lever, the slow running is provided for by a throttle adjustment on the carburetter.

The Ignition Timing Lever.

The ignition timing lever is fitted alongside the throttle lever in one of a number of ways ; sometimes both levers are placed on the steering column and not actually on the hand wheel, but another arrangement is to fit both levers to the facia board, in which case the steering wheel is free of any control fittings. The purpose of the timing lever is to adjust the instant at which the spark occurs with relation to the movement of the piston to suit the particular conditions of running, as correct timing has a bearing on efficiency of running. Some engines are much more sensitive to timing variations than are others.

7

HOW TO DRIVE A CAR.

In order to simplify driving so far as possible, many modern cars are fitted with mechanisms which automatically adjust the ignition timing in accordance with the requirements of the engine. In others, the automatic principle is used in conjunction with a manual control so that the driver still has some say as to the timing employed, although, if he wishes, he can leave everything to the discretion of the " robot."

Certain cars are fitted with a device called a mixture control, enabling the driver to get the most economical running, but the operation of this, together with that of the ignition and hand throttle controls, need not at this stage be considered. If such a mixture control is absent, it will be found that there is some simple device, such as a pull-out button or lever, which can be operated to give a richer mixture, temporarily, when starting the engine. The actual turning of the engine to effect a start is performed electrically by a motor brought into action by pushing a button ; it is important to release the button (allowing it to spring back) so soon as the engine gets under way.

Stopping the Engine. The Ignition Switch.

As the engine will continue to run slowly when the accelerator pedal is released, the usual means of stopping it is the ignition switch ; on some cars it is a separate fitting on the dash, and on others it is combined with the lighting switch. If the car has magneto ignition, the turning of the switch forms a connection between the magneto and the frame of the car and short circuits the current. If coil ignition is fitted, the switch breaks the circuit just as an ordinary lighting switch does. In either case, by putting the switch to the " off " position the ignition is cut off and the engine stops. Obviously, to start again the switch must be put to " on "—a simple point, but it is surprising how many novices will use the starter button again and again in vain before noticing that they have neglected to switch the ignition on.

You have sat in the car and depressed the various pedals, pulled the hand brake on and off, and waggled the gear control. You have a fairly good idea of where these various controls are placed, so we will leave the car for a moment and pass on to things which the new driver must do or know before he is fit to be allowed on the road.

Getting a Driving Licence.

No person is allowed to drive a car on a public highway without a driving licence. This can be obtained for 5s. from the borough or county council offices. The applicant must be at least 17 years of age. Driving licences, which remain in force 12 months from date of issue, are obtained in London at the County Hall, Westminster. Anyone can obtain the licence, after filling in a form which includes a declaration as to physical fitness, by payment of the fee. In addition to possessing a driving licence, the driver must know by heart the rules of the road. Some of these are definite laws, while others are customs dating back so many years that they are universally accepted, and have latterly been brought together in permanent form in the official "Highway Code." As mentioned on a later page, this edition is going to press at a time when a new Bill is before Parliament, which contains proposals for a driving test to precede the granting of a driving licence.

It is only by a policy of give and take that harmony can be maintained between the various users of a public highway. Never assume, therefore, that you are entitled to any more room than anybody else (taking the size of the vehicle, of course, into consideration). Most of these rules and customs will be pointed out in a later chapter. In Great Britain, all vehicle drivers keep to the left of the road. To overtake someone, you should draw out towards the centre of the road, resuming your left if anyone wishes to overtake you or if anybody coming towards you wishes to get past. Even while learning, it is as well to remember that you should put your right hand out if pulling out suddenly towards the middle of the road to overtake another vehicle.

If you have your driving licence, have learnt the position of the various controls, and have grasped the fundamental rules of the road, you are about ready for your first driving lesson.

While many teachers believe that the novice should start by getting away from a standstill and changing up through the gears, this is giving the learner rather a lot to think about at once. It will be found very much easier if, after a good run round with an experienced

A car can best be controlled when the driver sits close to the wheel, with his hands holding the rim in the positions shown.

driver whose every movement has been closely watched, the car be slowed down to a walk and seats changed without stopping the vehicle. This can be done quite easily on most cars, especially as the driver can hold the wheel all the time until the pupil is safely in the driving seat. For this operation, however, and for the ensuing initiation into driving a car it is essential to choose a quiet, straight and level road, so that the novice is not *flustered* by traffic, corners or gradients.

Now you find yourself actually holding the steering wheel of a moving car on the road, your right foot operating the accelerator pedal to control the speed. In case you wish to stop, all you have to do is to press down the clutch pedal with the left foot and simultaneously move your right foot from the accelerator pedal to the brake pedal, depressing the latter and releasing the former. Do not make the mistake of trying to go too fast. Any fool can drive fast: it is in handling the car at slow speeds than most skill is called for. If you want to steer to the right, turn the wheel to the right, i.e., clockwise. Steering to the left, you do exactly the reverse. This may seem very elementary, but a great many learners have an extraordinary propensity towards turning the wheel the wrong way.

You will probably find at first that you over-correct errors in steering ; that is to say, if the car, following the camber of the road, starts pulling to the left, you will turn the wheel too much when trying to resume a straight path, and so your first half-mile or so will very likely be a series of zigzags. Providing there is no one else on the road, or that you can keep from zigzagging when there *is* someone, there is no need to be alarmed. Very soon you will find just how light a touch on the wheel is necessary to keep the car straight.

How to Hold the Steering Wheel.

An experienced driver never keeps his car straight by rigidly holding the steering wheel so that it simply cannot deviate. Actually, he allows his wrists to be perfectly

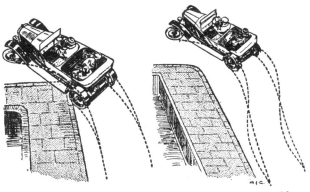

When a corner is negotiated, the rear wheels cut inside the path taken by the front wheels. If the driver fails to allow for this he will overrun the kerb.

flexible, correcting the slightest tendency of the vehicle to run to the left or right by almost imperceptible movements. The " feel " of the steering wheel does not really take long to acquire. Steering on deserted country roads is easy enough ; there are generally few kerbs at right-angle bends, nor corners of walls projecting, very hard and angular, at sharp turnings.

When turning to the left do not do so too sharply, as otherwise you may take the near (left) side back wheel over the kerb or scrape the running boards or rear wing on the corner of the wall. The reason is that, when taking a very sharp bend, the back wheels cut slightly across the arc described by the front ones, and the tail of the vehicle "cuts the corner." So before turning to the left, swing out a little towards the middle

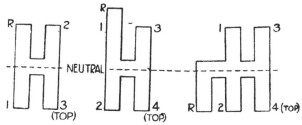

Three common arrangements for the gear positions : (Left) in a three-speed gearbox; (centre) a four-speed box with reverse obtained by going through the first-speed position ; (right) a four-speed layout with a separate reverse slot.

of the road, which will give your back wheels more room. When turning to the right there is more room, but make a practice of "following round" the left-hand kerb, i.e., do not cut across the corner, as this will take you on to the wrong side of the road in the path of oncoming vehicles.

When the art of steering has been mastered by evolution on a level surface, you should practise bringing the car to a standstill without stopping the engine. This, as was explained to you just before you took over the wheel, simply consists in taking the foot off the accelerator pedal, putting the clutch out by depressing the clutch pedal, and letting the car run to a standstill. If it will not stop soon enough, a light touch can be given to the brake pedal. You can, of course, stop the car by simply putting on the brake if you are not going fast, but then you will also stop the engine. When the car has been brought to a stop you do *not* need to press the pedals down for an indefinite time ; disconnect the engine, therefore, by moving the gear lever into the central (neutral) position, after which you can release the clutch pedal and apply the hand brake to prevent the car from moving.

Learning to Change Gear.

Now that you can steer the car confidently, both on straight and winding roads, and can bring it gently to a standstill without a jerk and without stopping the engine,

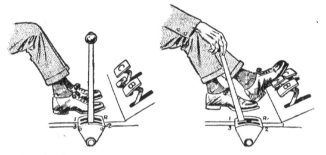

Starting from rest ; the gear lever is shown on the right for simplicity. (Left) gear lever in neutral. (Right) clutch pedal (C) depressed and first gear engaged.

the time is ripe to learn something about the gears. The best thing, perhaps, will be for you to change up through the gears and then be shown what has happened inside the gearbox at the time. We will assume, then, that the car is standing, with engine running, on the left-hand side of the road. The gear lever is in neutral, which is the middle position of the gate, and the clutch is in, that is to say, the pedal is up, the disconnection necessary to allow the engine to run being effected in the gearbox, as already explained. Either the notches for the various gears will be numbered or the driver will tell you their order ; three widely used arrangements are illustrated.

To engage first speed, which is the lowest gear, and, therefore, makes it easiest for the car to get away, depress the clutch pedal and put the gear lever into the notch for first speed. So far, you have not accelerated, but now, as you gently let in the clutch (i.e., let the pedal come up, using your heel on the floorboard as a fulcrum), you should gently accelerate by pressing down the small pedal. Then, if you have done it properly and balanced the movement nicely, the car will glide away.

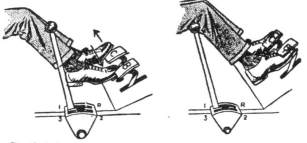

Starting from rest—continued: (Left) Accelerator gently depressed and the clutch pedal (C) released to move away. (Right) Car accelerating in first gear with the clutch pedal released.

Do not be surprised or downhearted if it gives a jerk and the engine stops; it only means that you have not accelerated quite enough, or that you have let in the clutch a little too quickly. A point to remember is that it is usually the last $\frac{1}{4}$ in. or so of movement, as the pedal comes up, which counts. Try again, releasing the pedal very, very gently during this final stage of movement. On the other hand, do not be frightened if the car suddenly leaps forward and starts rushing up the road. You are not going really fast; it is only the engine running fast on low gear that gives this impression. Take your right foot off the accelerator, declutch with the left foot, and make another attempt. What you have done in this case, of course, is to accelerate too violently. The engine should not audibly be " raced up " or accelerated to any extent while the clutch is being let in. You can spend quite a profitable half-hour in starting and stopping, until you can get away from a standstill without the slightest fuss or jerk and without stopping the engine. Do not try to accelerate the engine before declutching to put the gear in the first-speed notch, or the gear will probably make horrid noises and will not go in easily.

HOW TO DRIVE A CAR.

Changing Up from First to Second Gear.

So far so good, if you can make a satisfactory start. But you obviously cannot go on using first speed. For one thing, it is slow, and, for another, the engine is turning over unnecessarily fast. So, having brought the car to a standstill, and, while the clutch is still out, placed the gear lever in the neutral position, you can try changing up into higher speeds, starting away as before, but as soon as the car is comfortably moving and has gone a few yards on low gear, decelerate (i.e., slow down the engine), declutch (i.e., press down the clutch pedal) once more, then place the gear lever in the second-speed position. There is no need to get "fluffed" about this. Take your time and remember how you are doing it.

If the car is fitted with the ordinary type of three-speed gearbox (see illustration) the change up from first to second gear will involve moving the gear lever across to the right, through the central gap in the gate, before moving it forwards into the second-gear position. There is usually a catch to prevent it from going straight forward into the reverse notch. You will find that the easiest way is to exert both a sideways and a forward pressure on the gear lever, which will cause it to slip sideways quite readily through the gap on its way from the first-speed notch to the second-speed notch.

Almost every make of gearbox has its idiosyncrasies, and you will find that with some it is desirable to put the lever straight into the next speed notch so soon as you have declutched, while on others you must pause for quite an appreciable time before doing so. If you get your instructor to change a few times, listening to the beat of the engine to get an idea of how it has slowed down before next gear is engaged, and if you have also got to know about how long you should pause (long enough, say, to count two or three), you will find the manœuvre much easier. Having got into second gear, you change up to the next in a similar way as regards the manipulation of the pedals, but the gear lever will now have to be pulled back instead of pushed forwards to get it into the required notch.

HOW TO DRIVE A CAR.

In each case, to change up you decelerate, declutch, put the gear lever in the next notch (with a short pause in neutral), and let in the clutch once more, subsequently accelerating. A clicking sound when so doing generally denotes an attempt to change up too fast; while if you wait too long there will be the most alarming noises, by which the gearbox tells you you are ill-treating it. If this should happen, give the accelerator pedal a smart dab down with the clutch in and the gear lever in neutral. This will speed up the engine and enable the gears to engage when the clutch is let in once more. Above all, if you get flustered and the gears are making noises, do not continue to haul on the gear lever, but declutch and allow the car to come to a standstill. Then start, quietly, all over again.

Practice Necessary.

A certain amount of practice is almost sure to be necessary before you can get away from a standstill, changing up through all the gears smoothly and without noise; but, having once mastered the process, you will have more confidence, knowing that you can, at any rate, start well. At this stage you will probably still be driving over fairly level roads, so that if you are stopped for any reason you can always bring the car to a standstill, placing the gear lever in neutral; then, when the road is clear, you can start off again by engaging first speed and changing up through the gears.

The reverse gear is engaged only when the car is at a standstill, the process being much the same as when starting off in first (bottom) gear. As a rule, however, there is a catch which must be operated before the lever can be moved into the reverse slot, this being provided to safeguard the driver against accidentally attempting to engage reverse when the car is moving forwards.

Avoiding a Bad Habit.

If you find a great difficulty in manipulating the gear lever and experience a strong desire to look downwards —a bad habit which should be avoided—it is quite a good plan to devote a little time to practice with the car at a standstill. To do this, "chock" the front wheels with bricks and jack up one of the rear wheels clear of the road ; owing to the action of the differential in the back axle, it is only necessary to lift one wheel instead of both. Then start the engine and practise changing gear at your ease, remembering, however, that the free rear wheel is spinning round, so that onlookers should keep clear of it! This method can also be used for practising changing down, i.e., changing from a high gear to a lower one ; but the procedure required is more complicated than that necessary for changing up and cannot be grasped without some knowledge of the con- struction of the gearbox. We will, therefore, defer the description to the next chapter.

Handling the New Transmission Systems.

From the foregoing explanation you will realize that it is not too easy a matter to get the "hang" of gear changing on an ordinary car. For this reason a number of new transmissions have made their appearance in recent years, and are finding their way on to current cars in increasing numbers at the time that this edition of "How to Drive a Car" is in preparation. Conse- quently, the work would not be complete without some reference to the driving methods employed in the case of these new mechanisms.

The Free Wheel.

The free wheel is a device resembling the mechanism of the same name employed on a bicycle, in that it per- mits the vehicle to go on coasting forwards with the engine idling, just as a bicycle can run ahead when the rider ceases to pedal. More economical running results, but the most important advantage is marked ease of gear changing. For example, when changing down on a free-wheel car, double declutching (an operation de- scribed in Chapter II) is quite unnecessary ; all that you have to do is to release the accelerator pedal, pause for

B

about half a second for the engine to slow down, and then push the gear lever straight through without even declutching. So soon as it has gone home, "rev." the engine again to pick up the drive. It will be understood that the free wheel will not allow the car to drive the engine, and, consequently, so soon as the throttle is closed, the engine slows to idling speed. From this it follows that the braking action of the engine is lost.

Changing Up.

Changing up on a free-wheel car is much the same as on an ordinary car, with one important exception, viz., that the slight pause required must be made before touching the gear lever, and not with the gear lever in neutral. Your procedure, therefore, is to declutch and release the accelerator pedal simultaneously, pause half a second, and then pull the gear lever straight into its next position. In some cars it is not even necessary to declutch.

Every free-wheel device embodies a means by which it can be rendered inoperative so that the driver may regain the use of the engine as a brake in emergencies. It is important to note that in most cases the locking device should on no account be operated until the engine has first been revved up to take the drive. This is because a great deal of damage might be done by locking the free wheel with the car running fast and the engine idling. When you first start driving a free-wheel car you will find it advisable to put in a little practice with the locking arrangement so as to be quite *au fait* with its use should an emergency arise. Do not forget, however, that with the free wheel locked you cannot change gear so easily.

Self-changing Gearbox.

A special form of transmission, known as the Wilson self-changing gearbox, was pioneered by Messrs. Armstrong Siddeley some years ago and has since been adopted by many other makers.

Instead of the ordinary gear lever, there is a short lever on a quadrant above (or below) the steering wheel, which can be set in any position while the car is in motion. Setting the lever has no immediate effect, but the next time the clutch pedal is depressed the gears will change themselves according to the position in which the lever has been placed. A certain amount of discretion is, of course, required, although the operation of the device is so easy, because it would be highly inadvis-

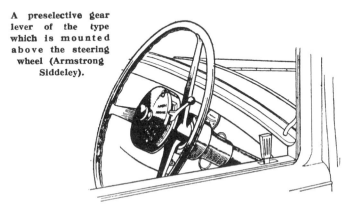

A preselective gear lever of the type which is mounted above the steering wheel (Armstrong Siddeley).

able (for example) to attempt to change straight from top to bottom gear with the car running at a considerable speed. Otherwise, gear changing is simplicity itself, the process being simply to set the lever and then declutch, keeping the throttle wide open for a quick change.

The "Silent Third" System.

With the combined objects of rendering the gears more silent and of facilitating the process of gear changing, many gearboxes are now designed on what is known either as the "twin-top" or the "silent-third" system. Four forward speeds are usually provided; of these the highest, or top gear, is, as usual, a direct and silent drive. "Third speed," the next down the scale of ratios, which is more widely used than any other, is provided by special constant-mesh gears with helical teeth. Such teeth run very quietly, and, consequently, the driver is as good as provided with two "top" gears. Furthermore, the gears are easily brought into action by dog clutches, as will be explained towards the end of the next chapter.

Synchromesh Gearboxes.

The widespread use of the "twin-top" type of gearbox led to a further simplification, known as synchromesh, which was first adopted by the Vauxhall Co. in England, and has since become widely employed. The toothed parts, known as "dogs," which move into engagement when the gear lever is shifted, are guarded by small cones; matters are so arranged that the cones make contact before the dogs reach one another. The friction between the cones then synchronizes their speeds (and, with them, the speeds of the dogs) before the teeth move into mesh.

With this system the driver has only to move the gear lever steadily from one position to the next, after declutching; undue pressure should not be exerted as the cones may then have insufficient time in which to do their work and a clash will result from the premature meshing of the spinning teeth. In some types of synchromesh a mechanical check is provided in order to prevent too rapid a completion of the change; in most of the lower-priced cars, however, the responsibility rests with the driver. Whereas synchromesh is applied only to top and third speeds, in most cases, it is also used for three or even four gears by other makers.

Automatic Clutches.

From what has already been explained, it will be understood that a certain amount of skill is required to start a car smoothly on its way, particularly on hills, by the gentle engagement of the clutch while the accelerator is employed to speed the engine. For this reason certain car makers have developed automatic systems of one kind and another. One of the most. important is the Daimler fluid flywheel: an automatic hydraulic coupling which disengages of itself whenever the engine speed drops below a certain low level. Thus a car to which this device is fitted can be stopped "in gear" without stalling the engine ; furthermore, to restart it is only necessary to open the throttle, as the recoupling effect is also automatic and is perfectly smooth in action. Such a device is naturally a great help in traffic and/or in hilly districts.

Certain other car manufacturers are employing orthodox clutches combined with special mechanisms designed to disengage the clutch automatically when the accelerator is released (or when the engine speed is sufficiently reduced) ; conversely, when the accelerator is depressed, smooth engagement of the clutch follows without attention from the driver. At the time of writing many experiments are proceeding on these and other lines, but the majority of the cars on the road are still equipped with foot-controlled friction clutches.

CHAPTER II.

What Happens in the Gearbox. Types of Transmission. How to Change Down and Double Declutch. "Running-in" a New Engine.

It is assumed that you have become proficient in the starting and stopping of a car and have obtained sufficient practice with the steering to make you confident of driving the car successfully for some distance entirely alone. This you might very probably be able to do, but if you came across a really steep hill you might have some difficulty in surmounting it on top gear, and so should learn now how to change down so as to provide a lower gear for the engine, which will enable an easier climb to be made.

Climbing a Hill.

The easiest way of all is to climb so far as you can on top gear, then, when the car has almost come to a standstill, declutch, put the gear lever in the notch for the next lowest speed, letting in the clutch immediately, although gradually accelerating meanwhile. Although this is the easiest way, it is by no means the best, chiefly because it allows the speed of the engine to die down, and as a motorcar power unit develops more and more power according to the rate at which the crankshaft is revolving, it is desirable to change down while the engine is still running moderately fast and is thus developing more power.

Although many competent drivers know very little about the mechanism through which the engine drives the rear wheels, you will find that a grasp of the essentials not only adds to the interest of car ownership, but also helps you to obtain the best performance. However, those readers who prefer to take the mechanism for granted can pass straight on to Chapter III.

HOW TO DRIVE A CAR.

An easy way to understand the transmission system of a car, as it is called, is to compare it with the mechanism of a bicycle. In each case the object is to convey power to the rear wheel or wheels. In the bicycle, this is done by means of toothed wheels and a chain ; in the car it is effected by the clutch, gearbox, propeller shaft and rear-axle gears, as shown by a drawing reproduced. The

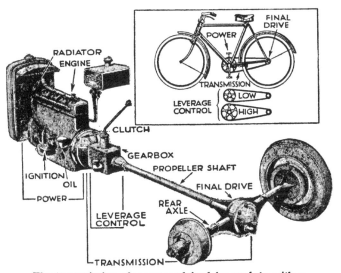

The transmission of a car explained by analogy with a bicycle. The gearbox provides, in effect, a variable leverage between the engine and the rear wheels.

clutch, as already explained, enables the driver to dis-connect the engine at will ; the final drive in the rear axle need not concern us.

We are left with the gearbox, which, in effect, pro-vides a variable leverage between the engine and the rear wheels. Referring again to a bicycle, the gear can be "lowered" by using a smaller sprocket on the pedal crank ; this means that the pedals will turn more rapidly than before in relation to the speed of the rear wheel. Similarly, in a car, the lower the gear the faster the engine will turn for a given road speed. Usually, four forward gears are provided, and in a typical case the engine speeds corresponding with a road speed of 20 m.p.h. may be 1,200 revolutions per minute on "top" (the highest gear), 1,800 r.p.m. on "third," 2,800 r.p.m. on "second," and about 4,000 r.p.m. on "first" (the lowest gear).

Now let us take the lid off the gearbox in order to find out how these results are obtained. A view of a complete set of gears will be found on page 28, but as this is rather confusing we will commence with just a part of the mechanism—that which is used for the top and third gears of this typical four-speed gearbox. This is shown in simplified form on the opposite page.

The shaft on the right, marked X, is driven by the engine through the clutch. In line with it, but free to turn at a different speed, there is a mainshaft (Y), which drives the rear wheels of the car through the propeller shaft and back axle mechanism. Lower down, in the gearbox, there is a layshaft (Z).

These shafts are connected by toothed wheels called gears. When the engine is running, with the clutch engaged, shaft X is rotating and, through gears A and B, is causing shaft Z to turn. Consequently, gears C and D must also rotate, but as the latter is loosely mounted it produces no driving effect upon the mainshaft (Y).

We now come to the function of the sliding member which is mounted on a series of grooves cut in the mainshaft. This part is controlled by the gear lever and takes up a central position when the lever is in neutral. The mainshaft (and, with it, the rear wheels) is then able to remain stationary whether or not the engine is running.

When the gear lever is placed in the top-gear position the sliding member is moved to the right, as shown. A series of teeth, called dogs, then become interlocked and so enable the first shaft (X) to drive the mainshaft (Y) directly. The gears and the layshaft (Z) merely rotate idly.

Moving the lever from "top" to "third" results in shifting the sliding member to the left. The dogs employed for top gear are thereby disconnected and, after passing through the neutral position, the sliding member engages with a second set of dogs, or teeth, formed in one piece with the gear D. Power is then conveyed indirectly from the first shaft (X) through gears (A and B) to the layshaft (Z), and thence back again through further gears (C and D) to the mainshaft (Y), and so to the rear wheels. Owing to the sizes chosen for the gears, the engine speed must now be a great deal higher than

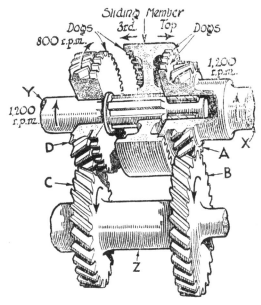

The parts employed to obtain top gear and third gear in a four-speed gearbox. In the position shown the drive is direct between shafts X and Y. The gears are idling, the fourth wheel (D) being freely mounted, so that it can turn at a speed differing from that of the shaft (Y).

before if the mainshaft (Y) is to run at an undiminished rate.

Suppose, for example, that top gear is engaged and that, with the car running at about 20 m.p.h., the engine is making 1,200 revolutions per minute (r.p.m.), the mainshaft (Y), being directly coupled to shaft X, turns at the same speed (1,200 r.p.m.), as indicated on the drawing.

Owing to the varying sizes of the gears used the idling gear (D) will be turning at a much slower rate—probably about 800 r.p.m.

Here lies the whole difficulty of changing down into a lower gear. If the sliding member is simply shifted from one position to the other, you will be attempting to interlock teeth moving at 1,200 r.p.m. with teeth turning at only two-thirds of this speed ; a clash and (probably) damage to the teeth will result. The obvious solution is to synchronize the tooth speeds before attempting to engage them.

How to "Double Declutch."

Before describing "synchromesh"—a mechanism designed to bring the teeth to equal speeds automatically— it will be as well to explain the method which the skilful driver can employ to ensure a quiet change. This method is known as "double declutching."

Taking the speeds and gears as already described, the problem is to change quietly from top to third with the car running at 20 m.p.h. First, the clutch should be disengaged (breaking the connection between the engine and the gearbox), and the gear lever moved into neutral ; the sliding member is thereby centralized, disconnecting shaft X from shaft Y. While this is being done the accelerator is released.

Secondly, engage the clutch and depress the accelerator. The engine speed will then increase and, with it, the speed of shaft X. Shaft Y will continue to rotate at 1,200 r.p.m., as it is driven by the rear wheels ; actually, it will slow down (with the car) to a slight extent while the change of gear is being made. The trick consists in revving the engine, while in neutral, to an extent just sufficient to bring the fourth of the gears (D) to the same speed as the mainshaft (Y). In other words, the engine speed must be increased to about 1,800 r.p.m.

Finally, the clutch is again disengaged and the gear lever shifted into the third-speed position. If the engine revs. have been properly judged, the teeth will engage quietly; if not, they will clash together and may refuse to mesh. In the latter event, you must not get flustered, jabbing the gear lever vindictively; just allow the car to come to rest and then commence all over again.

Let us just run over the movements involved in double declutching without reference to the "innards" of the gearbox. These are:—

(1) Accelerator (right foot) up; clutch pedal (left foot) down; gear lever shifted into neutral.

(2) Clutch pedal up, accelerator down, engine revved to a speed about $1\frac{1}{2}$ times its former rate of revolution.

(3) Clutch pedal down, pressure on accelerator eased to avoid over-revving, gear lever shifted into "third."

Do not practise this at too high a road speed until it has been thoroughly mastered, otherwise you may damage the teeth badly by a faulty change. The pedal action can be practised with the car stationary until it can be done without conscious effort. When you have learnt to "change down" quietly by this method, you will find it possible to achieve a still quicker change by holding the accelerator down throughout, just easing the pressure slightly towards the finish.

Exactly the same procedure is adopted when changing down into the second or first gears, but, of course, such changes will only be attempted at low road speeds.

Synchromesh.

The object of the synchromesh mechanism, now employed on so many popular cars, is to synchronize the speeds of the dogs prior to their engagement; the driver is thus relieved of the somewhat tricky job of double declutching. Close inspection of the drawing of a typical four-speed synchromesh gearbox which we reproduce will show that top and third gears are selected by sliding a member, to the right or left respectively, along the mainshaft, as in the simple mechanism already described. In addition, however, small cone clutches are fitted at each side which make contact before the dogs reach one another.

The procedure is as follows:—After declutching, you move the gear lever, shall we say, from top towards the third-speed position. Before its travel is completed you can feel, by holding it gently, a slight resistance as the cones make contact. They soon come to identical speeds, so that, after pausing for a very short interval

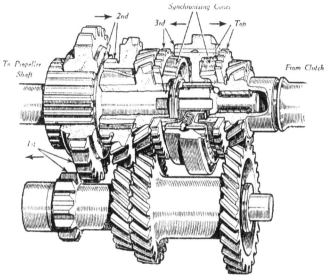

Gears and shafts of a typical four-speed synchromesh box (Austin Seven). The functions of the various parts are described in the text.

(varying from $\frac{1}{4}$ sec. to $\frac{3}{4}$ sec., according to the car, road speed, etc., in question), the gear lever can be pushed home with the assurance that the teeth will engage quietly.

Before re-engaging the clutch, however, you must increase the speed of the engine by depressing the accelerator. If you neglect this point the car will have to rev. the engine suddenly, as the clutch picks up the drive, and a pronounced shock or jerk may result which is both uncomfortable and bad for the transmission as a whole.

The action of synchromesh is limited to adjusting the tooth speeds for quiet engagement; it cannot take charge of the engine speed as well.

The drawing also shows the gears employed for second and first speeds, this being only one of the very many designs at present in use. As a rule, these gears are not fitted with synchromesh cones and, consequently, the double-declutching method of engagement must be used for a smart change down on a hill.

Before concluding this section, we may point out that another kind of synchromesh device is in use which embodies a positive check to prevent the hasty driver from completing the change before the cones have done their work. With this system the use of a heavy pressure on the gear lever merely expedites the change, whereas, with the simpler type of mechanism, it may clash the dogs into contact before their speeds have had time to become synchronized.

The Free Wheel.

That the method employed for changing gear is somewhat modified when a car is fitted with a free wheel was mentioned in Chapter I. Although the action of the free wheel makes gear changing a very simple operation, you should also master the gearbox with the free wheel locked, because, in hilly country, there will be occasions when you may cover many miles with the transmission in this locked condition. The method of control is then the same as that already described in this chapter.

The free wheel is a cam-and-roller device, fitted behind the gearbox; when the engine is driving the car the rollers are gripped by a wedge action and convey the power from the gearbox to the propeller shaft. So soon as the accelerator is released, however, the engine speed drops to an idle and the car coasts freely because the rollers will not grip when the turning effect is reversed, i.e., will not allow the rear wheels to drive the engine. Under coasting conditions, therefore, the propeller shaft continues to turn at undiminished speed, but the gears turn slowly, as they are connected to the idling engine.

Owing to the slow speed of the gears they can be changed, up or down, without even declutching, so long as the driver allows a short pause (after releasing the accelerator) to give the engine time to slow down. However, if changing straight from top to the second or first

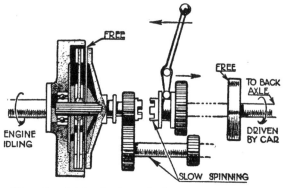

When the clutch of a free-wheel car is disengaged, the gearbox is isolated so that any gear can readily be brought into action.

speed (for example, after taking a sharp corner), it is usually best to declutch. The gearbox is then isolated and the gears are freed of all load.

The Self-changing Gearbox.

The gears employed in the self-changing gearbox work on what is known as the epicyclic principle, and run continually in mesh. The great advantage of this principle is that it enables gears to be selected by applying brakes within the gearbox instead of by sliding spinning toothed parts into mesh. The frictional grip of a brake band can be applied smoothly and progressively, so correcting small speed differences without shock.

There would be no point in describing the self-changing gearbox in detail, but you may be interested in an account of just one of the epicyclic units, viz., that which is employed for first speed. This is shown by two drawings, reproduced side by side. The central (sun) wheel, connected by a shaft to the engine, meshes with three planet gears fitted to a carrier, which is connected to the propeller shaft. A ring gear, or annulus, surrounds the planet gears and is fitted with a brake.

In the left-hand view the brake is free. The engine is idling, and with it the sun wheel; the planets turn on their spindles and cause the annulus to revolve slowly, but as their carrier remains stationary the car is left at rest.

Now suppose that the driver preselects first gear, and then, by depressing and gradually releasing the gear-change pedal, applies the brake to the rotating annulus. This pedal, incidentally, is operated by the left foot and

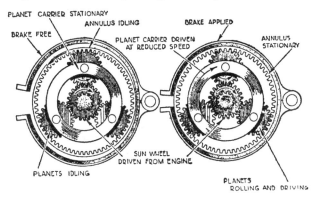

The parts of a simple epicyclic gear. (Left) Neutral position with the brake free. (Right) Brake applied to hold the annulus stationary, with power conveyed to the planet carrier at reduced speed.

replaces the normal clutch pedal. As the brake brings the annulus to a standstill, the continued rotation of the sun wheel forces the planets to roll round within the surrounding ring of teeth, so imparting a turning effect to their carrier which is conveyed to the rear wheels of the car.

Consequently, you will realize that the brake, in addition to selecting the gear, serves the function of a clutch by enabling the car to move off smoothly from a standstill. For this reason many cars fitted with this form of gearbox are not provided with a separate clutch.

Other brakes are used to bring the remaining gears into action ; in each case the gear is preselected by moving the lever to the required position, but no change occurs until the pedal is depressed and released.

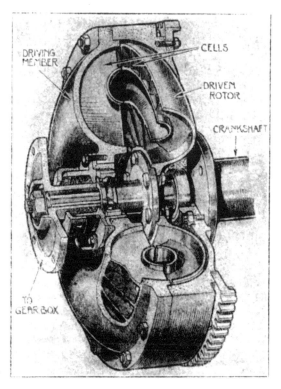

The Daimler fluid flywheel shown in section. There is no direct connection between the two rotors, but the one is enabled to drive the other through the medium of oil.

The Fluid Flywheel.

On three well-known British cars the self-changing gearbox is used in conjunction with a fluid flywheel, this combination being the subject of a patent. Changes of gear are made in the manner already described, but the brakes in the gearbox are not used when moving off from

HOW TO DRIVE A CAR.

rest. The necessary clutching action is performed auto-matically by the fluid flywheel which is placed between the gearbox and the engine.

This ingenious device consists of two cellular rotors, one driven by the engine and the other fitted to the shaft which drives the gearbox, working in a sealed casing filled with oil. So long as the speed is low—as, for ex-ample, when the engine is idling—the oil circulates freely through the cells and no power is transmitted. When the accelerator is depressed, the more rapid circulation of the oil produces a drag on the second rotor, which then commences to drive the car through whatever gear has been selected in the gearbox. As the speed rises the slip rapidly decreases, so that, under all normal running conditions, the rotors turn at practically identical speeds, although they are "connected" solely by the moving vortex of oil.

From the driver's point of view, the result is that the car can be stopped and restarted in gear merely by using the brakes and accelerator; it is not possible to stall the engine. Furthermore, by opening the throttle very slightly the car can be made to creep forward at a snail's pace—a material advantage in traffic.

Making Proper Use of the Gearbox.

It is assumed now that you have had sufficient practice in changing gear, both "up" and "down," to be able to carry out the manœuvre without undue trouble or hesitation. The next item to consider is when and how the gears should be used in order to obtain maximum efficiency from the car. Very many drivers have an absurd prejudice against changing gear at all. They will hang on to top gear until the overworked engine has started to labour and to knock before so much as think-ing about engaging a lower gear. By this time the speed of the car has dropped so much, as has that of the en-gine, that possibly the next lower gear is not sufficiently

33   c low to enable the hill to be climbed, and another drop to second or lower, according to whether three or four speeds are provided, is necessary.

Another type of driver may, perhaps, know how to change gear quite well, but he is for ever boasting how well his car will climb steep hills on top gear. Sooner will he climb slowly, with the engine turning over hardly fast enough to be efficient, than change down and make a really good climb. This craze for keeping to top gear at all costs has not a little to do with the poor performance and the rapid wear which develops in some engines.

Naturally, when and how one changes gear depends very greatly on the type of car. For instance, most large multi-cylinder cars of the luxury type, and, more particularly, almost any American six-cylinder car with any name at all, are specially designed to give a high output at very slow speeds, so that, once in top gear, it is seldom necessary to change down, except, of course, in very hilly country. At the other end of the scale there is the super-sports light car—fast, lively and equipped with an ultra-efficient power unit which has to be kept "revving" if the best performance is to be ensured.

Changing Down Early.

You will find that on most European cars of small or medium size it is not unusual for a good driver to change into a lower gear before he is actually on the hill at all. He knows that the faster his engine is running the more power it is developing. Therefore, a few yards, perhaps, from the start of a hill, he will change down, speed up the engine, and approach the hill with it running really fast and developing ample power. Thus the hill can be climbed quite fast and, what is more, with the greatest ease.

In between the large "woolly" six-cylinder and the high-efficiency small car is a wide range of vehicles of every kind of chassis weight and every type and size of engine. One soon finds out for oneself the characteristics, where hill-climbing is concerned, of one's own particular car.

HOW TO DRIVE A CAR.

Climbing Known and Unknown Hills.

Normally, perhaps, one speeds up the car, remaining in top gear when approaching a hill, either because one knows the acclivity and that it can be climbed with a rush, or else that one feels it is not very long, so can very

A good driver makes a practice of changing down early on a hill; particularly in a car of the sports type, fitted with a small engine which depends upon revs. for power output.

possibly be climbed on top gear. On a strange hill the motto of the driver of most cars should be "Change early." By this we do not mean to say that by a superb exhibition of double declutching he should engage second gear at 40 miles an hour. What we mean is that he should not let his engine practically die out before thinking of engaging a lower speed. So, as soon as a car slows down to 15 or 20 miles an hour, say, on top gear, he should change down, when he will very possibly find that he can climb a gradient actually faster on the lower gear ratio than on top, simply because the engine is working under so very much easier conditions.

HOW TO DRIVE A CAR.

A word as to the greatest speed at which a change down from, say, top to third should be made, after sufficient practice has given the driver a certain amount of skill in double declutching. The rule is not to change unless the speed on top gear has fallen a little below the speed which the driver knows the car can attain on the lower gear. Thus, if a four-speed car will do 40 m.p.h. on third, then the change from top to third should not be attempted until the speed on top gear has fallen to about 35 m.p.h. on a hill.

Changing Down in Traffic.

Nor is it only on hills that one should change to facili-tate the task of the engine. When it is decided to accelerate suddenly, the rapid change into a lower gear will make the increase in speed so much smoother and so much faster; while in traffic, instead of risking stop-ping the engine by causing it to run too slowly on top gear, to change into the next lower ratio will render the vehicle much more sensitive and much more con-trollable. At the same time, most of the luxury-type European or, perhaps, more ordinary American six-cylinder vehicles can be slowed literally to a walk with-out fear of the engine either stopping or losing in flexibility, so that it is only necessary to change down when the car has actually been brought to a stop and it is desired to start off again, or should better acceleration from a low speed be desired.

Do Not Slip the Clutch.

One of the worst "crimes" which the motorist can commit is to slip his clutch simply because he is too lazy to change gear. This is of little use on hills, chiefly be-cause slipping the clutch makes practically no difference to the torque or "twisting motion" of the wheels, in-stead of increasing it, as does the change into a lower gear; but in traffic, when running slowly, or when turn-ing the car round in a narrow space, slipping the clutch does, of course, result in a reduction in speed without stalling the engine. It is, of course, necessary to slip the clutch when getting away from a standstill, and clutches are designed to withstand this treatment for short periods of time without developing trouble; slipping produces considerable heat, however, and if continued for long will result in distorting some of the parts and damaging the lining, owing to the high temperature developed. The clutch may then become harsh in action or may refuse to grip at all.

For similar reasons, it is most unwise to get into the habit of resting your left foot continuously on the clutch pedal when driving your car, as even the weight of the foot reacting against the clutch spring may suffice to produce an unnoticed but continuous slip which is very damaging to the friction surfaces. Except when actually in use to operate the clutch, the left foot should rest on the floorboards beside the pedal, where it is ready for immediate action. After all, one does not consider it necessary to drive with the hand continuously holding the gear lever!

It is equally unwise to form the habit of slipping the brakes in the self-changing gearbox, as these grip by friction and are liable to damage by overheating, just as in the case of a clutch. Furthermore, although it is so easy to change gear with this type of box, you should pay some attention to the control of the accelerator, speeding the engine when changing down and allowing it to run more slowly when changing up. By so doing you will avoid shock and will make things easier for the gears and their brakes.

Running-in a New Car.

When, after learning to drive, you take delivery of a new car, you will want to learn more about the mechanism and how to maintain it in good condition. Helpful information is available in another Temple Press publication, "The Motor Manual," and useful articles are published regularly in *The Motor*.

Here it must suffice to give a few hints on what is called "running-in." By this is meant the process of running the new car carefully until all the moving parts are working smoothly—a process which may require anything from 500 miles to 1,000 miles.

The engine of a new car turns stiffly for two reasons: first, the bearings and pistons are fitted tightly, with minimum clearances, and, secondly, the working surfaces, however carefully machined, are actually marred by microscopic irregularities. In the course of running-in these surfaces are burnished until smooth and, as a result, the clearances increase; both these changes tend towards a reduction of friction.

Burnishing produces heat, and yet, if the surfaces are to be smoothed with reasonable rapidity, a certain amount of pressure is essential. Consequently, the first and most important requirement is an adequate supply of lubricant which will reduce friction and carry away the heat generated. Not only must the owner-driver maintain the proper level in the sump, but, in addition, it is essential that he should use a reasonably light oil of the right grade.

Particular care is necessary when starting a stiff engine from cold, because the oil is then thick and sluggish. It has to flow from the pump through a filter, a number of tiny passages and a series of tight bearings, before it is thrown into the cylinders by the rotating crankshaft; consequently very little oil reaches the bores and pistons during the first couple of minutes.

This is where the over-cautious owner is apt to make his first mistake: he sets the engine at much too low an idling speed when allowing it to warm up. In so doing he extends the time required and reduces the quantity of oil thrown into the bores. The proper speed is from 1,000 to 1,200 r.p.m., which can be roughly judged from the fact that it is about the rate at which the engine revolves when pulling the car at 20 m.p.h. on top.

Too low a working temperature does an engine far more harm than running too hot. The products of combustion condense on the cold walls of the cylinders and set up a corrosive action which has been shown to be one of the most likely causes of undue wear. Thermostat devices are of great assistance in this connection, a good alternative being the radiator muff.

The golden rule for running-in a new car on the road is to avoid sustained periods of hard work, which will raise the oil temperature to an unsafe figure. Provided that this is remembered, short bursts of speed, at intervals, will be found advantageous. Otherwise, general running can be done with an engine speed not greater than 2,000 r.p.m., representing about 33 m.p.h. on top and 21 m.p.h. on the third gear.

On the other hand, while over-revving is harmful, the engine should not be allowed to labour at full throttle. It is, therefore, better to change down on a stiff hill than to hang on to top gear, always provided that an excessive speed is not maintained.

After 500 miles have been covered it must not be assumed that the engine has suddenly become transformed into a free-running unit. Care is still required, and the best method is to increase the load and speed bit by bit, with more frequent full-throttle periods, so that by the time 1,000 miles is reached the car is being quite freely used.

At this stage it is very important to have the filters cleaned, the sump thoroughly drained and to refill with fresh lubricant. The running-in process results in the abrasion of a certain amount of metallic dust which mixes with the oil and is harmful to the bearings.

The whole process is undoubtedly assisted by using one of the many special running-in compounds now available, which contain colloidal graphite in the form of tiny particles in suspension. The graphite forms a greasy film on the metal surfaces, safeguarding them from seizure and helping them to attain a smooth, long-wearing "skin."

CHAPTER III.

Using the Brakes Correctly. Descending Steep Hills. What to do in Emergencies. How to Correct Skids.

Now that the correct use of the clutch and gears has been mastered, it is time that the brakes be given a little consideration. On them depends, to a very large extent, the safety of driver and passengers. Without good brakes, the driver is in continual danger either of being faced with an emergency in which he must stop suddenly or have a collision ; or else he may find himself one day rushing at breakneck speed down a steep decline, unable to reduce the speed of his vehicle, with a, perhaps, very unpleasant fate awaiting him at a twist in the road or at the foot of the hill.

Always see that the brakes are properly adjusted. At the same time, do not adjust them too tightly or they will be '' on '' all the time, which does not do either the engine or chassis any good, besides making the car extremely sluggish. It is, therefore, advisable, after running the car for the first time following the adjustment of the brakes, to feel each drum in turn with the hand to make sure that none is hot. Binding brakes are a common cause of a high petrol consumption. The brakes should never be applied suddenly and violently, unless it is absolutely necessary, as the sudden gripping of the shoes on the drums is certainly not good for axles and transmission generally. Apply the brakes gently but firmly, reducing the pressure on the pedal or hand lever as the speed of the vehicle decreases, so that it comes to rest absolutely smoothly and without jerk. This is not only a matter of brakes, but a question of habit, and it is surprising to notice the difference in the life of the brake linings caused by variations in driving methods. With

40

careful usage, the linings of a medium-priced car should last for 15,000 to 20,000 miles without renewal.

Always Brake Gently.

Many who have driven for years bring a car to a standstill in such a way that its final drawing up takes the form of a jolt. This should never happen. The car should glide to a standstill as smoothly and as gently with the brakes applied as it would do if allowed to come to rest of its own accord with the gear lever in neutral. True, when using the brakes, it comes to rest very much sooner, but the whole point to remember is to carry out the braking *smoothly*. On slippery, greasy roads, sudden braking is still more dangerous, as it may result in a skid. After you have had one or two skids, providing you have learnt how to correct them, you will cease to hold them in very great awe ; but, to a beginner, the helpless feeling of skidding sideways is a most unpleasant experience. However, the whole question of skidding and stopping skids will be dealt with later. The main point now is that, if you brake heavily on a greasy road, you will very probably skid ; so the moral is '' Don't.''

Use of Hand Brake.

On modern cars the design is such that the pedal applies brakes to all four wheels and is the control which is normally used when the car is in motion ; the hand brake sometimes takes effect upon the rear wheels only and is then neither so safe nor so powerful in its retarding effects. In particular, the hand brake should not be employed on a greasy road, as the car is much more liable to skid when rear-wheel braked than when four-wheel braked.

The hand brake, then, is primarily intended to prevent the car from moving when parked and should be applied whenever the car is brought to a standstill. Even in a short traffic stop, apply the hand brake, because, should another vehicle run into your car from behind, the fact that the brake is '' on '' will probably prevent the car from being '' shoved '' forwards into a vehicle ahead.

HOW TO DRIVE A CAR.

Do not forget to release the hand brake before starting away.

Making a Start Uphill.

Skill in the use of the hand brake is required when restarting a car uphill from a standstill, and this is a procedure well worthy of practice. Before touching the brake, declutch and engage the lowest gear available. Next release the clutch pedal very gently with the left

Restarting on a steep hill; after engaging bottom gear the hand brake and clutch pedal should be released gently and simultaneously while the accelerator is depressed.

foot, accelerate the engine with the right foot, and simultaneously release the hand brake. After a little practice you will find that you can get away smoothly and without running back at all, the engine taking up the drive just at the moment that the brake is released. Initial practising should be carried out on a moderate gradient, because of the danger of running back on a steep slope.

Should the hand brake prove difficult to control, the foot brake can be used in much the same way; but, as the right foot is then occupied, the necessary acceleration of the engine must be carried out by means of the hand-throttle lever. If an automatic clutch is used these operations are simplified, as the driver has only to control the brake and the accelerator.

Restarting on a hill with a car equipped with the fluid flywheel is effected as follows:—Leaving the hand brake hard on, preselect and engage bottom gear; the fluid flywheel will allow the engine to continue running. Next, depress the accelerator until you can feel that the engine is trying to start the car, like a horse straining at the collar. Then, if you release the brake, the car will move off with no danger of running back.

On a very steep slope you may find that the smooth pull of the fluid flywheel is not sufficient to start the car. It is then necessary to use the gear-change pedal just as though it were a clutch pedal, in the fashion already described.

Descending Very Steep Hills.

When descending very steep hills, it is good practice to use the foot and hand brakes alternately, always provided that the hand brake operates a separate and independent set of shoes, which is not very frequently the case nowadays. Naturally, a good deal of heat is engendered by the frictional effort of braking, and using the two sets of brakes one at a time gives each a chance of cooling.

On a very steep hill, it may be found desirable to engage a lower gear, so forcing the engine to revolve rapidly and to act as a brake. This saves the ordinary transmission or wheel brakes. At the same time, this practice may lead to oiled-up plugs, so that difficulty may be experienced in climbing the next gradient. When this occurs, it is due to oil being sucked past the piston rings into the cylinders. An extra air inlet connected to the induction pipe is here a great boon, because the throttle can be closed, the air valve opened, and a stream of cool air drawn into the engine, which not only prevents the suction of oil into the combustion space, but also exercises a beneficial cooling effect.

Keep Control of the Car.

Above all, never let the car get up too much speed when descending a gradient. You should check it gradually, and have the feeling always that you have the car under perfect control. Remember that it is very much easier to stop a slow-moving car with the brake than one travelling at a breakneck pace.

In descending a hill, consider those who are coming towards you. Do not draw out to overtake another vehicle if there is a car coming up the hill, unless, of course, it is some distance away. For one thing, as on the level, it is "his road," and you have no right to pass whatever is in front of you until he has passed it and you ; for another thing, he may not have very much power in hand and may want to make the ascent as fast as possible and, therefore, should be given a free course in which to keep up his speed and thus get the best out of his engine. You should always, of course, keep well to your left on corners, especially so when descending a hill, as you never know when you might come face to face with some reckless driver taking the corners much too fast, and probably much too wide in consequence, in order to make a rapid climb.

Use " F.W.B." Sparingly.

Four-wheel brakes are one of the greatest factors of safety it is possible to have, owing to the decreased likelihood of skidding on the grease and the excellent retarding effect which they produce. You should not, however, get into the habit of "driving on the brakes," i.e., relying upon them entirely and leaving only a bare minimum of space in which to pull up. Rather should you look on four-wheel braking as a means of lengthening the life of brakes and brake linings, with, of course, the knowledge that, *should* an emergency arise, you can pull up with amazing rapidity, but never forget that the driver following you may not be able to pull up so quickly. Four-wheel brakes are no excuse for taking risks ; reliable as are most modern types, they *might* fail one day, so drive sensibly.

Using the Clutch When Braking.

The way in which the clutch pedal should be used when braking is not understood by many motorists.

HOW TO DRIVE A CAR.

In the ordinary course of slowing the car there is no need to touch the clutch pedal ; but, obviously, it must be depressed before the car comes to a stop or the engine will be stopped also. In actual fact, a car can be pulled up in a shorter distance if the clutch is "out" than if it is engaged, so that in an emergency both clutch and brake pedals should be depressed simultaneously. This does not hold good on a greasy road, however, as it is usually found that the car is less likely to skid when braked with the engine coupled to the rear wheels than when the clutch is disengaged.

Stopping the Car if the Brakes Fail on a Hill.

However well designed the brakes may be, there is always a slight possibility of an emergency arising through the car getting out of control either when ascending or descending a hill. It is only right, therefore, that we should consider what to do if the brakes for any reason failed on a hill.

When touring in a really hilly country it is not advisable to coast down steep gradients. To "coast" means to allow the car to run with the gear lever in neutral and the engine idling—or to "free wheel," on cars so fitted. Should you be coasting and require the engine as a brake, "rev" it to a speed corresponding to that of the car, declutch and engage top gear ; it is worth while to practise this on moderate slopes. The engine may, of course, have stopped during the descent, in which case the electric starter must first be used. With a free-wheel car coasting is done "in gear." To use the engine as a brake it is then necessary to "rev" it in a similar manner before operating the control which locks the free wheel. Should the car get out of control then, if there is a side turning which can be taken safely at the speed at which you are travelling and either continues level or goes uphill, the best thing you can do is to take it. It is also a good thing to know that if you hit an ordinary gate fair and square you can almost invariably knock it off its hinges without doing much damage to the car.

HOW TO DRIVE A CAR.

The Engine as a Brake.

If you tackle the situation in time, before the speed becomes very great, a powerful braking effect can be obtained from the engine by "revving" it up to the greatest possible extent with the clutch "in" and the gear in neutral, then engaging second, or even first gear if possible. This proceeding is also worthy of practice on the principle of "being prepared," and is, of course, greatly facilitated by synchromesh or the self-changing gearbox.

On a winding road with high banks it is desirable, immediately it is found that the speed of the car is becoming dangerous, to turn the steering wheel sharply and charge the bank head on. If this is done at a moderate speed no serious damage should result and the car is not likely to turn over. You should, of course, cross over to the right of the road before turning, so as to make quite sure that you hit the bank squarely. When your speed is not very great, you can often reduce it by driving the car so close to the bank or hedge that the friction on the wings or body may reduce the speed sufficiently. A scratched motorcar body is very much better than a mutilated human one.

It does not necessarily follow that a mechanical breakdown is the only cause of a car running away backwards when on a hill. You might, for instance, be driving up a severe gradient when a choked jet or what not might bring the car to a stop. It may happen then that when you put the gear lever in neutral you find the brakes are insufficiently powerful to prevent the vehicle running back. In such a case you should turn immediately, and before the car has had any chance of gathering speed, at right angles into the bank or, at any rate, across the road in some way. You should do this in just the same way as if the car were running away in a forward direction, that is, you should reverse to one side of the road, swing the car right over on full lock so as to hit the bank or kerb fair and square. Trying to run up the bank by approaching it backwards at an angle may result in capsizing the car, so should be avoided.

46

HOW TO DRIVE A CAR.

Skidding and Risks of Greasy Tramlines.

You have been warned that you might very possibly skid should you be so unwise as to apply the brakes fiercely on a greasy stretch of road ; another point to remember is that if the brakes are out of adjustment, so that a greater retarding force is acting on one wheel, or pair, than on the others, the car may tend to swerve or skid. There are other causes of skidding, the principal being too rapid acceleration, sudden swerves, or taking a bend or corner too fast, especially where the camber of the road happens to slope in the wrong direction. Nevertheless, it may well happen with the most careful driving that the car will do an occasional skid.

Although to the novice skidding is a terrifying experience, generally conveying an impression of absolute helplessness on the part of the driver, it is, if looked at from a common-sense point of view, nothing at which to be unduly alarmed. At the same time, having learnt how to correct skids, one should not take risks, for correcting a skid, in any case, usually requires a certain amount of room, and on a crowded road there might not be space enough to check a skid in time to avoid a collision.

Providing one is driving at a moderate speed and avoiding violent acceleration or braking, or sudden swerves to right or left, sideslips will be relatively rare on ordinary roads. But where the bugbear of the motorist—tramlines—occupies a portion of the highway it is possible that the wheels may catch on the slippery rails, so that movement of the steering wheel has little or no effect on the direction followed by the car. This is particularly troublesome if, as is usually the case with cars of 16 h.p. and over, the track of the wheels is such that they exactly fit the lines.

Keep the Wheels Out of the Rails.

The great point to remember when negotiating greasy tramlines is that every possible effort should be made to keep the wheels from getting into the rails at all. On an empty road this is not very difficult ; but in dense traffic, when one often has to traverse the lines to overtake some other vehicle, with one or both of the back wheels on the tramlines, the tail of the car will slither about ; if all four wheels happen to be on the rails at once, the car will quite possibly not answer to its steering wheel.

Cars differ very greatly in their propensity to follow tramlines, and only experience can guide you as to whether or not extreme caution is needed on any particular vehicle. It is worth noting that any car is safer if the tyres are kept at the recommended inflation pressures by regular attention. When crossing tramlines, a skid will very seldom be experienced if care be taken not to turn the steering wheel *when any one* of the wheels is on the rails. So that when crossing a tramway track make sure that the front and rear wheels are either across or in between the rails before turning the steering wheel. Tramlines will then cease to hold any terror for the novice.

If you should happen to get all four wheels into the tramlines, do not get alarmed or attempt to apply the brakes ; a sudden movement of the steering wheel, executed in a decisive manner, will pull the car out. But be ready to correct the steering immediately afterwards to avoid too violent a swerve.

How to Correct a Skid.

Skidding is the bugbear of the motoring novice, but once he learns how to correct a sideslip the terror vanishes. Consequently, it is well worth while to take the car to some deserted and slippery roads and there deliberately to cause skids and practise their correction— of course, at low speeds. When, for one cause or another, the car commences to skid, the steering wheel should be turned immediately in the direction of the skid ; that is to say, if the tail of the car skids to the left, the front wheels should be turned to the left as well. Sometimes, if a skid is commenced when driving fast, this immediate turning of the steering wheel will have the effect of causing the rear of the car to skid to the opposite side (to the right), so that it is then necessary to turn the steering wheel to the right to check *that* skid. However, providing the correcting movement of the wheel is not too brusque, it should be possible to correct a skid at ordinary speeds by a turn of the steering wheel in the right direction.

A fundamental law concerning the adhesion of the rear wheels of a car is that any turning effort to which they

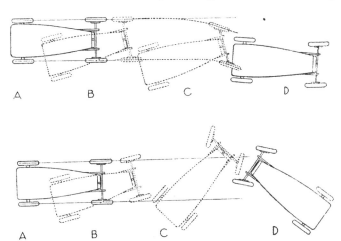

The course of a rear-wheel skid. (Top) The skid develops between stages A and B, whereupon the driver steers to the right (C), so causing the car to straighten out (D). (Bottom) In this case the skid develops as before (A, B), but the driver steers in the wrong direction (C), so accentuating the swing of the tail (D).

may be subject reduces their resistance to sideways movement; a sideslip, therefore, is most likely to occur during violent acceleration on an indirect gear or when braking. It follows that to apply the brakes harder when a skid commences is the worst possible thing to do. The correct procedure is to release the brakes immediately, leaving the accelerator pedal alone also until complete control of the car is regained. Even if you are sliding with wheels locked towards some obstacle, *release* the brakes until the wheels become free, and then apply them again, taking care not to do this too roughly.

Other Methods of Skid Correction.

A severe skid, in which the car might turn at right angles to the direction in which it is being driven, can be corrected very often by turning the steering wheel as before, giving, at the same time, a sharp tap to the foot brake. You will thus be deliberately causing a skid in the opposite direction to that which the car on its own has followed. Later on it is proposed to go into the matter of how skids can be artificially produced. You may say to yourself: '' Why on earth should I want to skid? It is horrible, anyhow.'' The answer is that one can sometimes, by a little judicious and intentional skidding, get out of what otherwise might prove a serious situation.

Certain modern road surfaces are open to criticism in that they become exceedingly slippery when wet, so that it is as well to go warily on a new and untried arterial road. In winter you may run suddenly on to a stretch of highway over which water has frozen into a film of ice ; even a gentle application of the brakes may then promote a skid. Experienced drivers form the excellent habit of keeping a watchful eye upon the road surface, particularly at night ; a change in its colour may mean that one has left a '' safe '' kind of surface for one that is far more slippery, demanding special caution.

When Ballast is Desirable.

Always remember, however, that if your car be a four-seater model, it will probably hold the road better under slippery conditions when fully loaded than when you are driving alone. The tread of the tyre has a certain amount of bearing on the disposition or otherwise of a car to skid. Old tyres, in which the treads have become practically smooth, do not obtain a good grip on the road. If muddy, greasy country lanes have to be included in many of your runs, you would be well advised to carry suitable tyre chains, as these permit of the wheels gripping the road when the tyres alone fail to do so. They are also quite invaluable when driving on snowy or frost-bound roads.

CHAPTER IV.

Manœuvring in Confined Spaces. Parking in the Street and in the Garage. How to Drive in Reverse.

It is a rather astonishing fact that many a driver of long experience, who is perfectly at home in a car on the open road, makes a hopeless muddle of placing it in a car park or garage. Manœuvring in confined spaces is quite an art in itself and one which you should acquire ; the presence of critical and, perhaps, sarcastic onlookers does not add to the driver's joy when he finds it quite a hopeless task to put the car in place—and then some nondescript garage hand will come forward and do the job with a few simple movements in a very short time! Here, as in other things, a knowledge of the correct methods is necessary, followed by practice.

Steering when Reversing.

As a first step, you should accustom yourself to the control of a car which is moving rearwards, the operation of steering it being then different from that which obtains when it is being driven forwards. In one of the earlier chapters it was pointed out how, if a corner be taken too close, the rear wheels will cut across the arc followed by the front wheels and thus run up the bank or over the kerb, or whatever happens to mark the boundary of the road on the bend. When proceeding backwards, exactly the reverse happens. The front wheels, instead of cutting across the arc followed by the rear wheels, actually cause the front of the car to travel in a part of a circle of greater radius than the path of the rear wheels.

An Example.

As an example, suppose the car to be standing very close to the kerb, with both front and rear wheels parallel to it. Now, if when starting away from a standstill in a forward direction you turn the steering wheel to the right, you will leave the kerb quite easily ; but if reversing and, owing to the necessity for leaving the immediate vicinity of the kerb, you still turn the steering wheel to the right, the front wheel on the side nearest the kerb will mount it, swinging the front of the car round over the footpath. Sometimes, of course, the wheel will not climb the kerb, and, unless you accelerate the engine very considerably, you will merely stop it.

Obviously, if you find yourself unable to get away in a forward direction when you are close and parallel to the kerb, you should reverse a short distance—a yard or two will generally suffice—with the front wheels absolutely straight and in line with those at the rear. In this way, so soon as you see that you have sufficient room to pull out without coming in contact with the vehicle in front of you, you can turn the steering wheel to the right and drive off.

Controlling a Car in Reverse.

The difficulty which many drivers experience when controlling a car in reverse is partly due to the fact that they do not adopt the best possible posture at the wheel. You should look backwards over the left shoulder, in the case of an open tourer, twisting round in the seat and holding the wheel with the right hand. The same practice holds good when looking rearwards through the windows of a closed car. In some cases it is more convenient to look out through the off-side window to follow the movements of the rear wing on that side, in which event you will find it more natural to hold the wheel with the left hand.

Do not, however, concentrate too much upon what the rear end of the car is doing ; always remember the way in which the front swings rapidly sideways when steered, so that, while you are busy watching the rear wing, the front wing may hit an obstruction.

Turning in the Road.

A manœuvre often required is to turn a car round in the width of a road, and a golden rule is never to attempt this in a busy thoroughfare, unless you are absolutely certain that the width from kerb to kerb is amply sufficient to permit the car to turn in one sweep without reversing. If you are uncertain, play for safety and make use of a side turning, preferably driving up it, turning in it, and then coming back to the main road again. If traffic permits, it is, however, quicker to back into the turning and then to drive away in the required direction. This is preferable to driving in forwards and then having to back out into the traffic stream.

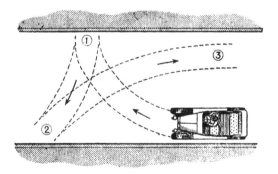

Turning a car in a narrow road: after driving forwards into position 1, the car is reversed (2) and can then be driven away (3).

When turning a car around in a quiet road, first drive up close to the near-side kerb and then, having looked to see that the coast is clear, turn the steering wheel fully to the right and drive the car across the road into a broadside position. Now engage reverse and back the car slowly away from the kerb, putting the steering "hard over" in the opposite direction as soon as possible. When the rear wheels reach the other kerb turn the steering once again and drive away forwards.

Many drivers make this a needlessly tedious operation, involving two or even more reverses, simply because they do not appreciate the need for making full use of the angle through which the front wheels can be turned.

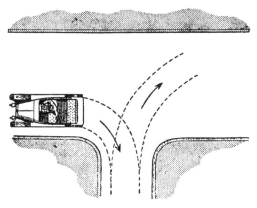

To avoid obstructing the traffic in a main road a side turning can be used for reversing, as shown by the arrows.

Another point is to swing the steering around as rapidly as possible after the car commences to move, otherwise valuable space is wasted with the car moving in a straight line.

Pulling Up Alongside a Kerb.

Many drivers, when stopping the car outside a shop or dwelling, place it so that the wheels often are so much as 18 ins. or a couple of feet from the kerb. This, of course, reduces to no mean extent the amount of room available for other users of the highway. Whenever you stop your car, therefore, make a point of getting as close to the kerb as possible. You can quite easily find how much room you should allow if you get out of your car and note by how much the wings overhang the outside edge of the tyre on the lower half of the wheel.

HOW TO DRIVE A CAR.

You can then with very little practice drive so that the tyre comes within an inch of the kerbstone. Obviously, you do not want to rub the tyres up against the kerb and thus scrape the covers, and that is possibly why you may be addicted to parking your car a clear foot or more from the pavement. It is all a matter of practice, and if one day when you have nothing to do you peg down a tape in a straight line at the roadside or in a quiet, open space, and practise bringing the car up with all wheels parallel to the tape and as near as possible to it without actually touching it, you will find your time has not been ill-spent, and that in a little while you will gain not only skill but confidence in the manœuvring of your car.

When Caution is Needed.

When pulling out behind a stationary vehicle, do so slowly ; for one thing, someone may be coming in the opposite direction and may not be able to pull up in time, and for another, unless you are very experienced, you might not have allowed quite sufficient room to clear the barrow, cart, or automobile which may happen to be in front of you. Therefore, draw out gently, watching the tip of your near-side wing (assuming that the car has been stopped at its proper side of the road) to see that it fully clears the obstruction. Remember that the tip of the wings is not over the point of contact between the tyre and the road, and that, consequently, it describes a wider arc than that followed by the wheel itself. This is a point often overlooked.

Manœuvring in a Garage.

The next point to deal with is the question of entering a public garage and manœuvring in it—a matter which looks simple, but which is, to the owner-driver, often a source of much worry.

The first step is to enter a garage through a narrow entrance ; this is merely a matter of practice, in order to acquire judgment as to the radius of the curve which the car will follow. Having practised until you can drive the car forwards through such an entrance, practise driving it through in reverse; an equally valuable acquirement. The golden rule when entering or manœuvring in a garage or parking space is to do everything as slowly as possible. Most attendants in such places have had long experience in the placing of cars and can tell the driver exactly which way to turn the steering wheel to reach the space allotted to him. However, no one likes to appear such a fool that he cannot even steer where he is told without having his front wheels pushed about by a mechanic, so the wise owner-driver will study the points involved and act up to them in future.

Practice in reversing is essential before one can hope to manœuvre a car safely in a confined space. You should be able to reduce your backward and forward manœuvres to the lowest possible amount. You will often notice that a skilful driver with one forward and one rearward sweep will get his car into the desired position, while an inexperienced driver will move to and fro a foot or two at a time an extraordinary number of times before being so placed that he or she can pull forwards or go back into the proper place. It is worth bearing in mind that when entering a garage at night it is generally much easier to drive in forwards, leaving the reversing out of a place until morning comes, and with it daylight. Some people quite unnecessarily make a fetish of always driving in in reverse.

Some Useful Pointers on Manœuvring a Car.

On entering the garage you should make a quick survey of the position of other vehicles, taking in at a glance the amount of manœuvring space you have at your disposal. If conditions are very restricted it may, of course, be necessary for you to edge backwards and forwards a few inches at a time until you can drive straight into position, but this is not really very often necessary. Remember what you were told in other parts of this book about the back wheels cutting corners when going forwards and the outward swing of the front wheels on a curve when a car is being steered in reverse. So if you are turning past a car in the garage it is unwise to assume that, because the front wheels get past, you will escape catching the rear wing on the front wing of a neighbouring vehicle.

In a Crowded Garage.

A crowded garage is, perhaps, the one place where you may be permitted to look at both sides of your car to see if you have enough room to get through. On the road, of course, you have learnt that it is dangerous rather than otherwise to try to look at both sides of your car at once. There is, in any case, no time so to do, so that the driver must develop the faculty of judging widths in relation to his car. In a garage, however, your own car and those of other clients may be so placed that the width of the space you have to go through varies considerably in the course of a foot or so. Therefore, proceed with the utmost care, stopping from time to time if you are very hemmed in to see if the front and back wings respectively would clear projections on other cars.

Where Reversing is Simplest.

It will be found that there are many occasions on which it is easier to reverse into a certain position than to drive into it in a forward direction. Experience and practice are really the best guides in this matter. However, generally speaking, where space is very restricted one can more often reverse into position than pull in forwards.

You should remember that, in order to reach the position in which it is desired to place a car in the garage, you may have to steer and actually take the car first of all where at first sight there is no need to, and certainly where you do not want to place it. For instance, you may find that, instead of steering straight into place, you have to describe an arc, getting as close to the wall as possible, and then swinging back on to the other lock so as to straighten up again. Remember that the front wheels travel in a greater arc than do those at the rear, and take full advantage of this fact.

HOW TO DRIVE A CAR.

An Everyday Problem.

Perhaps the clearest way to explain a simple garage problem will be by explanatory sketches. Supposing that in a garage or motor house already occupied by one

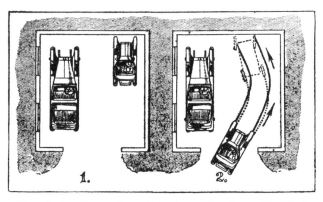

How to get the small car into the position shown (1). First, drive in as indicated. (2) Steer towards the wall and then away from it (see next illustration).

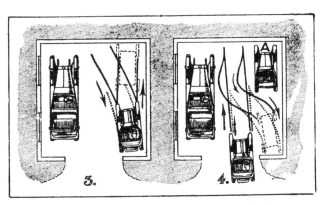

Next, reverse the car to the wall and then drive forwards (3). An alternative method is shown in the fourth illustration.

large car it is desired to put a smaller car close to the wall on the opposite side of the building, it would obviously not do to steer straight for the corner. If you do so you will find that the tail of your car is sticking out, taking up valuable floor space, and in order to get it as close to the wall as was the front of the car you would have to do a considerable amount of backward and forward shunting, which would waste a lot of time and possibly get you

How to drive forwards into a garage situated on a hill.

into no better position than you were at the commencement.

The best way to get into the position shown in the first illustration would be to steer for the right-hand wall,

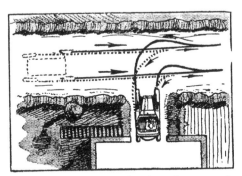

The alternative plan of reversing into the garage leaves
the car ready to drive away.

turning away from it so that the car finished up with the front wheels near the end wall and the car itself fairly well towards the middle of the garage. The next move would then be to reverse back into the right-hand corner near the door, straightening out the front wheels just before bringing the car to rest. Then, by driving forward, the vehicle can be placed exactly in the corner, as close as you like to the wall and absolutely parallel to it. The whole essence of the practice is to get the rear wheel close to the wall or car against which you desire to park ; it is easy then to make the front end swing sideways, but the rear wheels cannot readily be so moved.

Finding the Best Way.

The best ways of entering or leaving a garage obviously depend a great deal on the precise location of the motor house. For instance, if its approach is situated on a steep hill, it may be quite easy to drive up the hill and enter, but it may not be nearly so easy getting out, as that would mean reversing up the hill before being able to drive down. Also, when backing out of a narrow entrance, it is difficult to see whether a road is clear. It would be much wiser, therefore, to drive up the hill a little past the entrance to the garage and take a wide sweep backwards, reversing downhill into the garage.

Saving Time.

Coming out again you would then have a much better view of anything that was passing the gate at the time. Besides, it is often more necessary, particularly in the case of medical men, to whom minutes and even seconds are sometimes a matter of life or death, to be able to drive straight out without loss of time. It does not matter if putting the car back again takes a little longer in consequence.

Common Parking Problems.

Nowadays, parking places are so restricted in area in most towns that it is essential to know how to place a car in a confined space between others. The most common case is that in which there is a gap in a line of cars along a kerb and the gap is not very much longer than the car which is to be driven into it, parallel and close to the kerb.

If an attempt be made to steer forwards into the position, it will be found that the back of the car projects; yet many people make this mistake. What you should do is to drive a little way past the foremost of the two

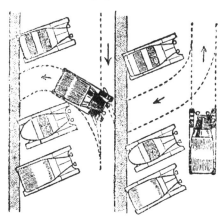

(Left) The wrong way to enter a diagonal parking place, involving risk of collision. (Right) It is usually much easier to reverse into place.

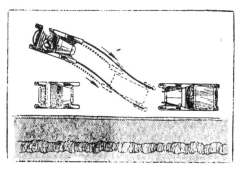

It is impossible to drive forwards into a space at the kerb, as the tail of the car will be left projecting.

cars, getting as close as possible to it, and then reversing first on one lock and then on the other so as to bring the tail of the car sharply round and just in front of the second vehicle. If it is not then in the correct position, it may only be necessary to pull forward two or three feet, when all four wheels will be parallel to the kerb.

If the street is crowded with traffic, making it inadvisable to reverse, a car can sometimes be driven in forwards by jumping the kerb, as shown in one of the illustrations. This is not, however, a practice to be generally recommended.

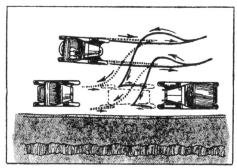

By reversing into place, and then driving forwards, the car can be parked neatly in line with the kerb.

Parking in Towns.

The ease or otherwise with which you may be able to drive into position in a motorcar park in a city street or open space depends largely on the method of parking

An alternative parking method which can be employed in a busy road, where reversing may be awkward. As this involves jumping the kerb it should not generally be used.

adopted. For instance, parallel parking with the cars at right angles to the kerb generally means that you have only to turn on full lock when just opposite the gap in which you propose to place the car, and subsequently to reverse into position.

HOW TO DRIVE A CAR.

Parking on the skew is easy or difficult according to the direction from which you approach the parking space. If, for instance, you are driving northwards up a road running north and south and the car park is on the left, and the rear parts of the cars against the kerb, so that their radiators are pointing slightly up the street —i.e., north-east—you need only drive a little past your position to be able to reverse on half-lock into position. On the other hand, if you are driving southwards, you would need to reverse through an arc, forming, as near as no matter, three parts of a circle, during which you would not only obstruct the passage of other traffic to no small extent, but would also risk catching the wings or running boards on the wings of the car next to you in the rank. A safe rule is always to approach a parking space from the direction in which you have to deviate to the least extent from the straight in order to get in ; this rule applies also when taking up a position in a herring-bone formation, such as is adopted in the middle of wide, open spaces and at some racecourse car parks.

Precautions when Parking.

You should, of course, always remember to leave the car with the hand brake on, no matter how level the parking space may seem to be ; also, if you are leaving the car in the late afternoon when darkness is likely to come on before you return, you should leave instructions with the A.A. or R.A.C. scout, or whoever is in charge of the park, how to switch on your side lamps. Remember that many parking places are governed by police regulations as to the direction which the parked cars must face, the maximum time they may be left unattended, and so forth. It is very tempting to lock the doors before leaving the car, but this should be avoided if there is anyone present to look after your car, as it entirely prevents the attendant from pushing it a few yards to enable someone else to get his car out in your absence.

Incidentally, when leaving a car by the roadside at night, you ought always to leave it on the side that it would normally occupy if proceeding along the road, so that the tail lamp is farthest from the kerb. This not only clearly defines your position to motorists approaching your car from the rear, but avoids confusing those coming in the opposite direction, who might not know on which side of the car to steer. Never, in any circumstances, leave your car unattended with the headlamps switched on ; they are then a potential source of dazzle to every other road user, waste a lot of current, and serve

If a hairpin bend is too acute to be negotiated in a single sweep, the car should be driven into the position shown and then reversed for a second attempt.

no useful purpose whatever. Some drivers carry a set of oil lamps for use when leaving the car parked for long periods after dark. This is not at all a bad idea, as it serves to economize the energy of the battery.

Where the side-lamp bulbs are rather powerful, leaving the car stationary with the engine switched off and the dynamo, therefore, not charging for several hours, may take so much current that, especially if the weather be cold and the oil in the engine gummy, the starter will not be able to get sufficient current to enable it to turn the engine round. Some car owners fit small stops on the starter or horn buttons to prevent tampering by mischievous boys.

Negotiating Hairpin Bends.

When touring a hilly country, especially if you forsake the beaten track and explore on your own the narrower by-ways, you may be confronted now and again by a really sharp hairpin bend. Sometimes the length of the car or a limited steering lock (which means the angle through which the front wheels can be turned) will prevent the bend being taken in one sweep. In this case it will be necessary to reverse into position for re-

It is impossible to negotiate a sharp bend by hugging the near side of the corner.

commencing the ascent after the angle in the road has been negotiated. If the corner be "cut," you will probably experience difficulty in reversing, owing to the fact that, when going backwards, the front wheels will try to climb the bank or go across the strip of grass on the inside of the bend. By taking the curve wide, however, you have very much more room in which to manœuvre the car in reverse gear, and will not find it nearly so difficult in consequence to make a comfortable restart.

CHAPTER V.

Driving in Towns: Trams and Traffic.

No matter how many miles you may have driven your car over country roads, your first journey through the thick traffic of a busy town is apt to be eventful; driving in traffic is, in fact, an art in itself, and with this we will deal in this chapter. Of all forms of urban traffic the tram is likely to give the most trouble to the new motorist: partly because of its impenetrable bulk, which enables it completely to hide other vehicles or pedestrians, and partly because the tram driver has no directional control but must always follow the lines. Then again, unlike any other vehicle, the tram sets down its passengers in the roadway, some distance from the safety of the kerb.

The engineer who plans the tramway system plays all sorts of pranks on unsuspecting road users. For instance, from time to time, for no apparent reason, he will cause the tramlines to switch over suddenly to the left or right, or at a slight narrowing of the road he will bring the two rails together, so that they interlace and run parallel for a space only six inches or so apart. Again, they may actually join at such a spot, in which case points come to add their quota to the irritation already caused, particularly to the unfortunate cyclist, by the original rails.

The Course of the Rails.

When following a tram it is as well, so far as is possible, to see what course the rails themselves take for some distance ahead. Generally speaking, where the tramlines occupy the centre of the roadway a tram is passed on its near side—i.e., on the left; but it is not unusual for the tram rails to swerve towards the left,

66

Trams and buses serve as most useful travelling route-indicators through towns if their destination boards are observed and the routes utilized as guides.

At night the illuminated tops of telegraph poles or
trees give warning of another car approaching.

so that there is no longer sufficient space between them and the near-side kerb to permit the passing of a car.   If you should be so careless as to overtake a tram just when it is following the rails to the left, you may be faced with the unpleasant alternatives of mounting the kerb or being crushed between the tram and, say, a lamp-post or pillar-box.

Especially is this likely to happen on corners, where the minimum radius of the curves the tram can take is too much for the streets.   In this case, tramlines which up to the bend have occupied the centre of the roadway will often, if it is a right-hand corner, suddenly swerve to the left, taking the corner very wide indeed, resuming

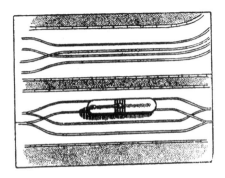

Two tramline layouts which are likely to trouble the unwary.

the centre once more on the other road.   There is another danger to be guarded against at such spots, this being that, even although there may appear to be ample room to pass a tramcar, judging by the rails, the tail of the tramcar itself may swing across in a wider arc, partially obstructing the thoroughfare.   In some districts central tram standards are used, and these provide another potential danger. If, owing to the presence of a slow-moving vehicle on the left of the road, and perhaps a tram coming to a standstill to allow for the alighting of some passenger, you pull out to the right, it is possible you may find yourself face to face with one of these standards.

Avoid "Cutting-in" Risks.

Of course, if there is no tram coming in the opposite direction, you can go on the outside of it, but the police are usually inclined to view this procedure as driving on the wrong side of the road, so a certain amount of discretion is required in the matter. In any case, it is most

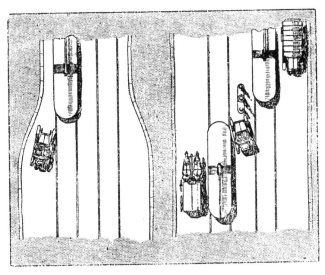

(Left) A sudden narrowing of the road may make it impossible to pass a tram on the near side. (Right) Central standards constitute a danger to the unwary.

unwise to dash past a tram and try to get back on the left of the road, cutting past the standard before the tram reaches it. It may result in your car being caught between the tram and the standard, with very unfortunate results. Similarly, a like risk is taken when trying to cut between two trams going in opposite directions. It may result in your car being cut in half, or, at any rate, sandwiched. It is difficult to estimate the speed at which a tram is approaching "head-on"—many travel at as much as 30 m.p.h.—so that "cutting-in" should be avoided as being a risky procedure.

Overtaking on the Left.

In the event of a tram having stopped and the road being full of passengers about to board it, you should, in towns where it is not considered an offence (and, of course, if traffic permits), overtake the tram on the off side. If you may not do this, it is far better to stop. After all, it does not take a minute to allow passengers to alight from or board the tram, and, even should you try to force your way through, you would almost certainly be confronted with an obstinate man or woman who would refuse to hurry. In any case, forcing your way

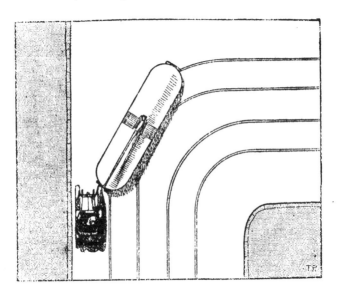

An overtaking car may be caught between the swinging end of a tram and the kerb.

past on the near side of the tram when the road is full of pedestrians is the kind of action which gives motorists a bad name, so that it is very much better not to do so.

Another point in connection with electric trams is that their magnetic brakes enable them to pull up exceedingly quickly, quite as quickly, as a matter of fact, as a car equipped with four-wheel brakes. The moral is: Do not follow close on the rear of a tram travelling fast down a busy street.

Rapid Acceleration of Tramcars.

Similarly, the acceleration of these great vehicles is really astonishingly good, and a speed as high as 25 m.p.h. can be reached in a very short time. Therefore, do not take it for granted that you can, by simply

When passing a bus stop one should be prepared for the last bus pulling out to overtake those in front.

accelerating, reach any point before the tram ahead of you, especially if it happens just then to be getting away from a standstill.

We have pointed out in an earlier chapter the danger of skidding on the tramlines when the road is wet. It only remains to mention that the difficulty of "seeing through" a tram constitutes another hazard. When passing a tram on the left, for example, remember that an (unseen) pedestrian may be running across in front of it from the off-side of the road. Similarly, a tram may hide another vehicle completely at a cross-road. Extreme caution is therefore the only safe rule to adopt.

HOW TO DRIVE A CAR.

Overtaking Motorbuses.

Passing on to another type of public vehicle—against which, however, the bitter reproaches levelled against trams cannot be raised—there are one or two points in connection with motor omnibuses that should be realized. There is, as a rule, no more courteous, and often no more skilful, driver than he who pilots a gargantuan motorbus.

Generally speaking, he keeps to his left, not obstructing the way to faster traffic, or, if he does hold the centre of the road, he almost invariably gives way the moment he hears the horn of an overtaking vehicle. At the same time, like every other vehicle on the road, motorbuses need watching. A sharp tug on the bell-cord from a passenger wishing to alight, and the driver will often swoop over to the left of the road and come to a standstill. Practically always, however, he will have put out his hand as a warning, so the bus driver should be watched carefully for signals. When passing a stop where two or three, or even more, omnibuses may be congregated, it is as well to see, for instance, that the last in the queue, having taken on his passengers quicker than those in front, does not pull out suddenly with a broad and majestic sweep into the thoroughfare.

Taxi Tricks.

Another public-service vehicle that needs *very* careful attention, now that we are talking of traffic driving, is the taxicab driver. Now, these may be divided into two classes. One is the youngish man, who is paying for his cab by instalments, and is, therefore, very careful of it, and, on the whole, a fairly sensible and well-behaved road user, and the other is the ex-cabby, who does not care the proverbial two hoots for anybody. The latter will, without the slightest hesitation, turn completely round in the road immediately in front of a private car doing 30 m.p.h. with never a sign of his intention. He will also suddenly swerve across to the extreme right to drop his fare or pick up another, or, having swerved well out in the middle of the road and given every indication that he is about to turn to the right, he will turn to the left, thus planting himself broadside on straight in the path of any motorist who is so unwise as to jump to the conclusion that because he goes well over to the right he is about to take a turning on that side. As a general rule, it is not safe to rely upon the signals made by a taxi driver; he will often turn off to the left after holding out his right hand.

Taxi drivers are apt to swerve across the road suddenly to pick up a fare.

In very many cases awkward situations in traffic could have been avoided by the judicious use of the horn. Of course, no one wishes to punctuate his progress down a busy street with a series of toots, but should you be about to overtake a driver of whose intentions you are uncertain, then give a hoot of warning in order that he may realize that another vehicle is about to pass.

The Horsed-vehicle Danger.

The drivers of horsed vehicles, although the slowest, are quite frequently the most reckless. For instance, if a motorist comes out of a narrow turning into a main road at ten miles an hour, he may be prosecuted, and quite rightly too, for dangerous driving, but if a fast-trotting horsed van comes out of the same turning at twelve miles an hour, not one official takes any notice at all, and yet not only can any car travelling at that speed be pulled up quicker than a horse-drawn vehicle, but the driver is able to see any approaching danger quicker than that of a horse-drawn vehicle, who is sitting, because of the length of the animal between the shafts, several feet farther back. In an anxiety to save the horses from unnecessary stopping and starting the police are, perhaps, often unduly sympathetic towards the driver of a horse and van, allowing him to take liberties which endanger other road users.

In busy districts the drivers of horse vehicles often emerge from side turnings at an excessive speed.

A fault of which van drivers (and private coachmen, too) are often guilty is that they seldom make any signals, although there is a time-honoured set of whip signals for their use. The most common fault is, of course, to pull the horse's head sharply round to the right, apparently under the blissful assumption that any motorcar, even if it be travelling at 40 miles an hour, can pull up in a bonnet's length, and then they call out rude remarks to the unfortunate motorist, who, seeking to avert what appears to be an almost imminent calamity, skids sideways across the road, missing the horse's head by an inch, when, in actual fact, the fault is entirely the carter's.

Riders of pedal cycles are often the source of much worry to the motorist. One would think that the rider of a bicycle would be so very conscious of the flimsiness of his machine and his exposure in the event of a collision that he would be particularly careful to observe scrupulously the rules of the road, but, as a matter of fact, he is often the most reckless of road users.

An entire disregard of the necessity for giving signals and an ability to swerve from a straight course at an instant's notice are the chief faults of the bicyclist. Consequently, it is never safe to assume that he will pursue a straight path, and a gentle hoot before overtaking him is always advisable.

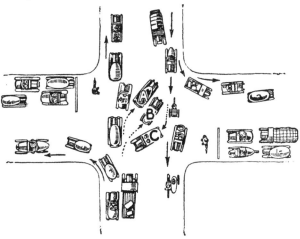

How to negotiate a busy crossing. Cars A and B are stationary, waiting for a chance to turn to the right, and car C is about to proceed down the opposite thoroughfare. The cars are so placed as not to obstruct the main flow of traffic.

Point-duty Police.

In all large towns the traffic at the major crossings is controlled by one or more police, and many of the busiest are now so complex—particularly in London—that the stranger should take particular care to watch the constables' signals. Even in the case of a straightforward crossing where two roads intersect at right angles, there are certain rules to observe in order that dislocation may be reduced to a minimum. For example, you should keep as close to the left kerb as possible when approaching the crossing if you intend eventually to turn off to the left. If the traffic is held up and you are at the front, then it is best to give a gentle hoot and signal your intention to the constable before turning off to the left, even if the way is perfectly clear.

If you wish to turn off to the right across the approaching traffic stream then draw over to the centre of the road slowly, with right arm extended, so that following vehicles may be aware of your intention and may avoid being held up by passing to the left of your car. Finally, come to a stop and await the constable's signal to proceed across to the right.

At all crossings pedestrians are apt to make a tortuous way through the held-up vehicles, and will often continue to do so as the traffic moves off; care is needed, therefore, to avoid them. When "held up" always endeavour to place your car neatly in line with the kerb so as to allow other vehicles to pack in closely; stopping in an awkward diagonal position is seldom of any advantage to the driver concerned and is a source of inconvenience and annoyance to others. It has become increasingly common recently to place white lines running across at right angles from the near-side kerb at a crossing; if you are the first to arrive after the constable has walked across to hold up the stream, be careful not to allow the front wheels of the car to overshoot this line.

"Circuses" and One-way Streets.

As the volume of traffic increases in the towns various schemes are adopted by the authorities to keep it flowing; the most important innovation in this direction of recent years is the "circus" system, now used at many important centres. The principle of the circus is to allow the traffic to circle a central island in one direction only—usually clockwise—as indicated in the drawing reproduced. Where a road enters such a circus a prominent notice, "Turn left," is usually displayed and arrows are marked on the road surface.

The usual rule of the road regarding "Keep to the left" is abrogated when negotiating a circus or a one-way street, the traffic following round a circus until each vehicle reaches the road at which it is to branch off. Thus a car entering the circus shown by the road (A) would have to be driven round the island for two-thirds of a circle to reach the road (B). During part of the

A typical one-way circus with the traffic all moving clockwise. To proceed from street A to street B involves driving diagonally across the traffic stream at point C.

journey the driver would naturally keep close to the island in order to avoid traffic entering from intermediate roads, and he must therefore be careful at or about the point marked (C), as here he must proceed diagonally across the traffic stream in order to gain the near side of road (B).

Automatic Traffic Signals.

In many towns throughout Britain the traffic is con-trolled by automatic signals at various important road intersections. A special sign carrying a disc and the words "Automatic traffic signals ahead" is placed on all main roads where they enter a town in which such signals are used, but, in any case, it is wise to be on the look-out for them when driving in a town with which you are not familiar.

The signals themselves may be four in number—two on each of the roads which intersect—or there may be a central standard carrying signals facing in four directions. The systems vary to some extent, but three lights are always used: red (stop), amber (caution) and green (go). A very important point is that if you have been held up by the red signal, you must not commence to move upon receiving the amber signal, but must await the green light.

Filtering to the left against the red signal is permissible only when a green arrow is illuminated.

The short period during which amber is shown is expressly intended for the purpose of giving a moving vehicle on the other road time to get across or time in which to stop, according to its position. Similarly, if the signal changes from green to amber as you approach a crossing do not attempt to dash over, unless you are very close to the intersection—too close to stop comfortably. Remember that very soon that amber signal is going to give place to the red light, whereupon many impatient people on the other road will leap forward in response to a green light! Automatic signals are safe only when treated with proper respect.

Not all towns employ the same rules with regard to turning off to the left or right at a crossing which is automatically controlled. As regards turning to the left, there is no difficulty if green be shown as one approaches the crossing, but the red signal means "stop," and the safest plan is to wait for it to change before turning off. In some cases a green arrow (pointing left) is illuminated simultaneously with the red signal, and it is then permissible to turn off.

To turn right, await the green signal and then move into the middle of the crossing. If no cars are approaching, it is usually permissible to complete the turn there and then, but in some towns the police expect you to remain in the centre until the signals change once again. The safest rule is, therefore, to wait if you are in any doubt.

CHAPTER VI.

Driving on Country Roads and Main Highways: Night-time Motoring: Use of the Horn and Driving Mirror.

Just as town driving needs thought and practice, so is skill of special kinds required for fast driving on main highways or the negotiation of the narrower and more obstructed country roads. Many of the former are relatively new arterial roads, in the making of which there have been unavoidable intersections with existing highways carrying heavy traffic, so that you should not be misled by the width and straightness of an arterial road into a belief that cross-road signs—a panel with a St. Andrew's cross in black surmounted by a red triangle—can be disregarded with impunity.

The most common mistake made by a novice who has just begun to "feel his feet" and increase the speed of his car on main roads is the passing of slower vehicles at the wrong times and places. Passing another car usually involves placing your own car well towards the off side, facing on-coming traffic, and this you should never do unless there is an ample sufficiency of clear road in view in which to complete the operation of passing and to regain the near side.

Many things may obstruct this sufficiency of clear road and render passing inadvisable or dangerous, so be patient rather than pushful; there may, for example, be a blind bend in the road ahead, a crossing, or a hump-backed bridge, any one of which may hide an approaching vehicle. And if you can see a vehicle approaching be careful not to under-estimate its speed; rather should you play for safety and allow ample time.

HOW TO DRIVE A CAR.

If you have been following another car for some time and an opportunity to pass suddenly presents itself, toot to warn the driver ahead and put out your hand decisively before pulling over to the off side ; a faster car behind may also be overtaking. That is where an efficient mirror is useful, a quick glance into which will

Although the old 10-mile speed limits have been abolished, it is essential to drive slowly and cautiously through villages.

show whether or not there is a car behind at close quarters. Central mirrors, reflecting through the rear window, are now very popular on saloon cars ; but remember that these have the defect of not revealing the presence of another car unless it is directly behind your own.

Special care is required when overtaking fast motor coaches, owing to their length and width ; their drivers are usually on the alert, and it is as well to make sure that they are aware of your intentions before commencing to pass. A courteous wave of the hand will give this information to you, but do not assume from this that you can rely upon a clear road ahead ; it is *your* business to see that overtaking is practicable, and you cannot safely depend upon anyone else in this respect.

On main roads most cars are being driven at fairly

high speeds, so that you must be careful to give an appropriate warning signal before making any abrupt change in the speed or direction of travel of your car. Do nothing suddenly. Turning off to the right demands special care ; slow down gradually and pull over to the centre of the road with arm extended as the turning is approached, making quite sure that no one is about to overtake before you actually swerve off to the right.

If you wish to stop for a time on a main road be careful to choose a spot in which your car forms the least possible obstruction to fast traffic ; for example, do not pull up on a bend in the road or near to a corner. Frequently there is a grass border along the edge of the road

Horses are often led on the right of the road.

on to which the car can be driven if the ground is not too soft to make this procedure inadvisable. In main-road driving at high speeds to be forewarned is to be forearmed, and some habits of observation which can be cultivated with advantage are described in a later chapter.

81 F

HOW TO DRIVE A CAR.

Many of the older main roads of Britain intersect villages fairly frequently, and these should be traversed with caution at reduced speed.

Various obstructions peculiar to country roads must next be described, but before proceeding it must be pointed out that on few of these roads are there any pavements, so that pedestrians must walk on the highway and will often show a strong disinclination to move, even when four or five abreast.

Herds of Cattle.

When meeting a herd of cattle or sheep it is generally best to stop the car altogether until they have passed. This will often be found quite as quick as trying to pick your way through moving animals, and thus obviates the possibility of anyone accusing you of driving into the sheep. Cattle drovers are by no means invariably competent. With cows, however, it is generally better to keep moving slowly, hooting, or, better still, shouting at them to get out of the way. More than once a cow has "barged" sideways into a stationary vehicle, seriously damaging a wing.

Country Roads at Night.

It is at night, however, that the greatest danger lurks on country roads. Cows, for instance, are not usually equipped with head and tail lamps, and it therefore depends on the power of the motorist's headlamps and his own good eyesight to pick them out in sufficient time. Of course, Nature provides most animals with light reflectors, which the cyclist has now been forced to fit, and these are their eyes. The first sight of a herd of animals on the roadway at night is generally a mass of twinkling lights somewhere in the indefinite distance. At first sight it may seem as if they are a cycling club out for their annual night run, coming down a distant hillside en masse. Closer investigation will probably prove them to be a dozen cows or so blinking at your headlamps.

Cats are very prone to lie in the middle of the road at night, and where they do not bound out of the way it is perfectly safe, as a rule, to drive either so that the animal passes unharmed under the car between the two wheels, or to steer to the right or left. A cat is, in this respect, often much more sensible than human beings, inasmuch as in the case of danger it stops where it is and makes no attempt to leap about the road.

The Unlighted Wagon.

The unlighted farm wagon is an ever-present source of danger, although, perhaps, even more dangerous is the timber wagon on which huge logs project rearwards 20 ft. or so beyond the tail lamp. The only safe rule, when driving at night, is never to exceed that speed at which it is possible to pull up in the length of a head-lamp beam. In daytime such objects as led horses, flocks of sheep or poultry, droves of cattle and so forth are not at all uncommon on the road. Every considera-tion should be given both to the animals and to the man or woman in charge of them. Remember that your car is always much more controllable than is a sheep or cow.

Bicyclists.

Many cyclists take pleasure in driving side by side several abreast and obstructing the road entirely to one line of traffic, often obstinately refusing to make way for those wishing to overtake them, so that if there is much traffic coming in the opposite direction—i.e., towards them—the pace of every other road user is set by a few slow cyclists talking as they ride. It is never safe to hoot and carry on at full speed, relying upon the cyclists to move to the near side, as in nine cases out of ten they will refuse so to do and leave you no room to pass them if a car is approaching.

Horses, when properly led, should keep to the right of the road, the person leading them being between them and other traffic. This rule dates back almost to time immemorial. Due allowance should always be made for the fact that the horses may be restive, and, when meeting led horses in a narrow country road, it is desir-able to avoid compelling the man in charge of the horses to halt his animals, even if to do so means taking to the right-hand side of the road: always provided that there is no "blind spot" ahead from which an oncoming car may emerge suddenly. This means, of course, that the horses, first and foremost, be allowed right of way, providing that this can safely be done.

Overtaking Sheep.

When overtaking sheep it is desirable first of all to sound the horn so as to warn whoever is in charge of the animals that the driver wishes to pass. The shepherd will probably keep the animals to one side and indicate the course the motorist should pursue. Care should, in

Lack of consideration when overtaking sheep may stampede them into some farmer's field.

any case, be taken not to force the sheep into a field or side road by any too sudden movements.

As regards chickens, these are in England fairly sensible and do not, in most parts of the country, go into the wild panics that characterize fowls on the Continent; also, in this country, the motorist who kills a fowl is liable for the cost of the bird. In France this is not so ; it is the poultry-keeper's fault if the fowl is so foolish as to stray under the wheels of a car. In the old days fowls were a much greater nuisance than they are now, so presumably hens now instruct their young as to the best way of dodging a motorcar. Ducks and geese are not met quite so often, but generally cause little trouble, as they are comparatively slow in their movements. Geese will sometimes stick in the middle of the road glaring indignantly at an approaching motorcar, but a blast of the horn will generally send them away uttering dignified protests.

As regards dogs, many motorists claim that they can be frightened away, as a rule, by a sharp hiss. Dodging small animals, although one always wishes to be as humane as possible, calls for a great amount of circumspection, for there have been many cases of fatal accidents due to cars skidding in frantic swerves to avoid running over a dog.

The Importance of Using the Horn Correctly.

To the comparatively inexperienced driver it may seem superfluous to devote a portion of this book to the operating of such a simple piece of mechanism as is the horn, but on the correct use of the warning device the safety of the driver and other road users very often depends. You may often see an unusually cautious driver punctuate his progress along the broad highway with a succession of hoots. Indeed, he will sound his horn on the slightest, and very often without any, provocation. Such unnecessary hooting is often aggravating to the general public and other road users, and tends in time to become disregarded by pedestrians, so that sounding the horn has no more effect than did the cries of " Wolf! Wolf! " uttered by the little boy in the fable.

To other road users sounding the horn would appear to be an urgent necessity regardless of road conditions, and this is certainly the view generally held by the police, as almost the first question they ask after an accident is: "Did you sound the horn?" At cross-roads and sharp corners it is, of course, always desirable to sound the horn, in order that you may give warning of your approach to anybody that might possibly be coming towards you from some quarter which you could not efficiently observe. But as regards hooting at all pedestrians on the road, a great deal of discretion must always be used.

When Not to Give Warning.

For instance, if some little way ahead you see a pedestrian step off the kerb, you would, of course, sound the horn to inform him that you are coming, in order that he may pause a moment before crossing the road, or, alternatively, keep his eyes upon you while he does cross the

In circumstances such as these it is usually best to apply the brakes and to steer behind the pedestrian, avoiding the use of the horn.

road. On the other hand, supposing somebody suddenly dashes off the kerb without the least warning just in front of you, it may prove the height of folly to sound the horn while the person is, say, on a level with the radiator. He will probably pause to see where the sound comes from, and in that fatal moment may get run down.

HOW TO DRIVE A CAR.

If the man, woman, or child should have the sense to run straight on, then, indeed, there would be no harm in sounding the horn, but by steering slightly behind them it is possible to get by without doing anything more serious than giving them a start, whereas were the hooter sounded they might turn round and attempt to run back—a manœuvre which it would obviously be impossible to execute in the time available.

Varying the Tone.

The loudness of the hooter ought to be varied, if possible, and in this connection it is noteworthy that noisy Klaxons are not allowed to be used in any French towns, although full use may be made of them on open country roads. Therefore, on all French cars a bulb horn is necessary for traversing cities, although it is true that the law allows for a very subdued-tone electric horn of the buzzer type, and some of the two-note electric horns now on the market fulfil the requirements of the regulations. The modern system of using two tuned high-frequency horns results in a note which is rather strident for use in towns. A switch can be obtained whereby the horns can be used singly or together at will.

A ferocious screech from a Klaxon may give some old lady heart failure, while, on the other hand, it is the only possible way to awaken a sleeping carter. Generally speaking, the noisy Klaxon is a too startling instrument for warning pedestrians, and should be reserved for informing traffic preceding that you wish to overtake it. The horn must always be kept in working order. Electric warning devices are, perhaps, the most popular, and these are, on the whole, very reliable. It sometimes happens, however, that they will not function when the button is depressed, although if pressure is kept applied to the button the horn may work when a bumpy stretch of road is traversed. This is often due, as in the case of motor-driven horns, to the commutator being dirty and coming to rest with the brushes on a bad place. Alternatively, the toothed wheel which makes contact with the stud on the diaphragm may become stuck at one point.

HOW TO DRIVE A CAR.

Don't Squeeze the Bulb Suddenly.

It should be remembered also that a bulb horn will seldom work if the bulb be squeezed very suddenly; either it will make no sound at all or will emit a wheezy groan with no carrying power. Remember, therefore, that even in an emergency the bulb must be squeezed firmly but steadily, with no more haste than you would use at any other time. Correctly handling a bulb horn is generally a matter of practice, and one soon gets used to it.

Night-time Motoring.

We mentioned earlier in this chapter the need for care at night on country roads in view of the unlighted obstructions which may be present; it remains to give some advice concerning another difficulty, which is caused by undue light instead of the lack of it—namely, glare from the headlamps of oncoming cars. Luckily, this dazzle nuisance is gradually becoming less acute, as more and more cars are being fitted with some device whereby the headlamp beams can be dimmed or dipped when other vehicles are encountered. Very seldom is it wise to "black out," however—i.e., entirely to switch off the headlamps.

When meeting other traffic at night, if the car being met has very powerful headlights and its driver does not bring an anti-dazzle device into operation, invariably slow down and go slowly immediately after passing the other car, until such time as a clear outlook on the road is again attained. The light is frequently so dazzling as partially to cause one to lose the ability of seeing such objects as cyclists or small vans which may be a short distance in front on the left-hand side of the road; one should always be careful in passing a car under these conditions.

Never use powerful headlights in town driving excepting when you actually need them. It is ludicrous, of course, to use electric headlamps in such a place as London, and it is a considerable annoyance to other people, and of little service to the user. With suitable qualification, such procedure might be reasonably prohibited. A very occasional exception arises when traversing certain streets which are known for their extraordinary danger, through the multitude of children living and playing therein, and in such cases headlights are undoubtedly a safety medium, being an additional warning to any children who are in the habit of rushing from the path into the road. In all ordinary circumstances, however, it is advisable to refrain from using the headlights for town work.

Anyone who intends to do much driving at night should pay attention to the correct focusing of his headlamps ; a lamp which is out of adjustment gives poor illumination and dazzles other drivers. A dipping device can now be obtained very cheaply and should be fitted if possible ; particularly valuable are the types in which the beams are not only dipped but are also caused to swing towards the near side, so lighting the edge of the road very effectively even in the face of glaring non-dipped headlamps. It is particularly necessary to look out for an unlighted obstacle when negotiating a left-hand bend with the headlamps shining straight ahead, leaving a dark patch on the near side. Auxiliary lamps can be obtained which give an anti-dazzle beam of short range but wide spread. Another type can be coupled to the steering gear so as to swivel automatically on curves.

CHAPTER VII.

Road Sense: Anticipating Emergencies and Cultivating Observation. Driving in Wet Weather: Skidding. The Art of Towing. Driving in Fog.

As you will now have had some driving experience, you may have acquired that indefinable but very useful quality known as road sense. This is acquired in a certain degree by most drivers as time goes on, through experience and the cultivation of habits of observation, but true road sense tends to be an inborn characteristic, which comes out within a very short time of learning to drive, or not at all. It is, as it were, a kind of clairvoyance of the road.

A man or woman with well-developed road sense often knows intuitively of dangers before there is any audible or visible sign of their approach. Such a driver may slow down unaccountably on a dark road, knowing instinctively that there is danger ahead, and, sure enough, he may find that had he gone on at his previous speed he would have had great difficulty in getting round some dangerous corner. Similarly, he knows, very often before he sees or hears the slightest sign of it, that he is going to meet another vehicle round a corner, and almost always that premonition proves to be true.

However, road sense can, to some extent, be developed, and, consequently, you should take care to be as observant as possible. Just as to a woodcraftsman the sudden flight of a flock of birds or the stirring of grass portends the presence of some living creature, so will a

90

distant puff of dust or the tip of a coachman's whip seen over a wall signify the approach of traffic.

A Mental Process.

Analysed critically, road sense can generally be found to be a distinct mental process. For instance, a skilful driver, seeing a cow by the side of the road, may often continue at unabated speed because he has already, unconsciously, made up his mind what to do in any eventuality, and so can act in the fraction of a second, often necessary to avoid an accident, without having to take thought. Some drivers appear to posses this sense from the first moment of taking over a car; others only acquire it after years of experience.

A child will often run across the road in response to a call from someone who is unaware that a car is approaching.

Examined closely, the mental process involved is something like the following: The driver thinks to himself, albeit unconsciously: "Now if that beast wanders over to the right of the road with the average speed of its species, I shall have room, by hugging the near side of the road, to get round behind it. If, on the other hand, it strays into the middle of the road and stops there, in my present position there is room for me to stop in any case. If I am a little closer, I can safely rely on my four-wheel brakes to pull me up, but if the animal should take up that traffic-obstructing position at the very last moment, I can still clear it by taking to the grass, which at the point in question is obviously firm and short.''

Anticipating the Unexpected.

The driver has, of course, thought out on similar lines every other possible manœuvre which the beast might or might not be expected to perform, and so, whatever happens, he does the right thing at the right second. The same unconscious thoughts are put into practice in any other eventuality. Every kind of animal, every driver of a horse or motor vehicle, every pedestrian, receives similar thought.

It might seem at first sight as if motor driving would then become a nerve-racking exercise in mind training, so that at the end of a longish run the owner-driver would be in a condition approaching a nervous breakdown. In actual practice, however, such reflections are purely automatic and absolutely subconscious, so that no strain whatever is experienced. Indeed, nine out of ten drivers would not know that they were reasoning, in an extraordinarily abbreviated space of time, on the lines we have suggested. If you asked them why they did this or that, the chances are they would reply, ''I don't know ; I just *do* it.''

Experience is, of course, very important ; similar situations recur again and again, and the brain of the practised driver becomes accustomed to jumping to the correct deduction from various sets of observations. For example, if he runs up behind a vehicle which is being driven slowly and hesitatingly along in the centre of a main road, he will take every precaution before passing, knowing by previous experience that the driver of that vehicle is searching for a turning or house which may cause him to dive to the right or left suddenly and without warning. These instances could be multiplied indefinitely, but are better left for you to learn on the road ; only, exercise caution during the learning process, and do not rely implicitly upon any other vehicle or pedestrian to continue a straight course without being warned of your presence.

HOW TO DRIVE A CAR.

Cultivating Observation.

The motorist can possess no more valuable asset than the ability to take in a complete view of the road conditions ahead of him in any second or fraction of a second. We all know the game introduced at children's parties, and sometimes on other occasions, when a tray of assorted objects is brought into the room, shown to the assembled company for one minute and then taken

If a pedestrian hesitates and looks to the left, it is a clear indication that a car is likely to emerge from the side road.

away. The guests are then asked to write down from memory a list of the objects on the tray. This is really an exercise in training the eyes, and it is not without practical utility from the motorists' point of view. Although the driver of a car is not called upon to state on his return from a drive exactly what the conditions were at any given point of the route at the time of his passage, he should be able at any time to appreciate fully, not only exactly what is on the road, but what is likely to be on the road.

Dangers of a " Narrow Outlook."

Some people have a very limited field of vision ; that is to say, they look straight ahead. Not a few accidents have been due to other vehicles charging a motorcar in the side at the very moment when it is passing them.

HOW TO DRIVE A CAR.

Such a contretemps could often be avoided if the driver possessed the gift of being able to see sideways as well as forward. Generally speaking, any such breadth of vision is acquired with practice. From force of habit the motor driver finds himself watching, not only both sides of the road at a point 50 yards or so ahead, but also taking in anything that is on the pavement on a line with his front wheels. The need for a broad field of vision is especially necessary when town driving, when one may be passing down a wide thoroughfare or crossing a wide open space from which side turnings debouch in various directions. For a man with a very narrow field of vision driving under such conditions would compel him to proceed at a very low speed, sounding the horn continuously. This is a state of things which automatically "rattles" the nerves, causes loss of self-confidence and leads to bad driving.

Estimating Speeds.

A combination of experience and inborn road sense enables the driver to estimate to a nicety exactly when and where any vehicle or person would cross the path of the car. In this way, by proceeding fast or slowly, according to the conditions, he could pick his way through the most populous thoroughfare without causing inconvenience to other road users, and very often without having to stop his car at all.

A wide range of observation also adds considerably to the joys of motoring in the country. Unless you have a fairly broad field of vision all that you see is the road, unless, of course, you deliberately turn your head to one side to admire the scenery, in which case you might very likely hit something. If you can see what is on each side of you without taking your eyes off your path you will enjoy motoring all the more and yet without running any undue risks. If a good general impression of the surrounding countryside can be obtained by glancing at it out of the corners of one's eyes while really looking straight ahead, it is equally true that by turning the head to catch a glimpse of this or that beautiful feature of the landscape, the experienced motorist is able to observe the course being followed by the car out of the tail of his eye.

Eye and Brain Should Act Together.

After all, motoring, if it merely consists of rushing along the roads with one's gaze fixed on the tarred surface, soon becomes boring. One of the greatest charms of automobilism is the opportunities it brings for seeing so much varied and interesting scenery. Colour is a great aid to observation, especially as so often a slight variation in the shade of a hedge or bank shows where a side turning, from which may issue some other vehicle, is situated.

Not only must different objects on the road or entering the road be seen clearly, but the eye must convey the message to the brain with the least possible delay. The speed with which this little piece of mental telegraphy takes place depends to a great extent upon the temperament of the driver. Often when the man at the wheel has apparently not seen an obstacle until quite close to it, it will be found that in actual fact his eyes have taken in whatever there is to be seen, but his brain has been too slow-moving to enable him to act up to it. The faster the speed at which the car is being driven the more important it is to appreciate the potential possibilities of any object on the road the very moment it is caught sight of. At high speeds there may be merely a fraction of a second in which to avoid a possible smash.

The Value of a Second.

At 30 m.p.h. a car is travelling at 44 ft. per second, so that by wasting a couple of seconds, first in observing and appreciating the importance of another vehicle, and, secondly, by bringing the brakes into action, the car will have covered a distance of 88 ft.—nearly 30 yards— which is not too close for many pedestrians to dash heedlessly in front of an approaching motorcar. Naturally, one should concentrate on those factors which are most likely to produce an accident. For instance, it is generally desirable to reduce speed wherever there are children about, as there is never any knowing whether, in response to some call from across the road, a child will not dash across the path of a swiftly approaching vehicle.

Road sense is merely a realization and understanding of common or garden signs, and the mind should be trained to watch for such signs and translate them into useful meanings.

Bus Route Indications.

When driving in traffic one should look *underneath* buses, so that one can observe the directions of the alighting passengers from their feet. Reflections in shop windows on corners give indication of what is approaching in the opposite direction. This, incidentally, is particularly useful at night. The actions of pedestrians are often very useful as an indication as to whether or not another car is likely to emerge from a side turning. If people are walking across the side road unconcernedly it is fairly safe to assume that no car is approaching; danger should be anticipated if the pedestrian stops and steps back to the pavement.

When on tour and driving in a strange country, if the nature of the road suddenly changes from good to mediocre, it is fairly safe to assume that one has encountered a local omnibus route, and a wary lookout should be kept on corners.

Incidentally, it is very interesting how one can always tell the regular omnibus routes from the rippled surface of the road. It gives a peculiar motion or feeling to the car that is obtained on no other road surface.

The contour or formation of the country often gives a clue as to what may be expected ahead. For example, if the road suddenly dips into a valley it is fairly safe to assume that there will be a stream of some sort in that valley and a bridge over it. In the majority of cases bridges have sudden approaches, and too heavy a foot should not be kept on the accelerator in consequence. "Hump-backed" bridges need particular care in negotiation.

HOW TO DRIVE A CAR.

Road sense when driving at night is particularly valuable. The wind, the stars, and the lights of other vehicles all give indication of movement on the road, just as the scared swirling of birds over a copse tells the hunter that there is movement beneath them.

Sky and Wind Indications.

When driving by night in strange country without a map, the North Star gives one a general indication of one's direction. If the sky is clouded, the wind serves the same purpose, for it very rarely veers to more than 30 degrees in anything up to six hours, unless the weather is particularly stormy. The illuminated tops of telegraph poles or trees give warning of the approach of another car at the cross-roads.

On a winding country road the smell of an exhaust, if noticed, indicates that there is an unseen motor coach or lorry round the next bend, while the shining green eyes of a dog tell the experienced motorist that there may be a pedestrian, cyclist, or even a flock of sheep a few hundred yards ahead.

As a rule, children, except the irritating kind who take pleasure in walking slowly in front of a fast-moving car to show their little friends how brave they are, are fairly sensible. It is generally sufficient to sound the horn, when they will wait until the car has passed before crossing the road. If the horn is not sounded, they generally assume either that you are going very slowly or that you are going to stop, and so do not trouble to hurry across the road. Dogs are quite sensible, as a rule, and will, if left to their own devices, get out of the way in plenty of time, but so often the frantic owner standing on the kerb and shrieking "Fido" will attract his attention at a crucial moment, so that he will run just where he should not, i.e., under the wheels of the car. Cats and chickens are not in the habit of coming when they are called, except at feeding time, so that there is really little need for anticipating any sudden movement so caused on the part of any other animal but a dog.

HOW TO DRIVE A CAR.

"Seeing Through" Vehicles.

Most vehicles, except, perhaps, a heavy furniture van or a tram, can be, so to speak, seen through ; that is to say, there is, in the case of many carts, plenty of space between the floorboards and the road, between the wheels and between the horse's legs, where quite a good view of the thoroughfare can be obtained. Also, when following a closed car, it is possible to see what is ahead by looking straight through the window at the back, through the screen and thus to the road beyond. Glancing under an approaching lorry will often reveal the legs of small boys hanging on behind, who might drop off and run in front of you, or the wheels of cyclists who might also choose to swing out at an inopportune moment.

When approaching cross-roads, deductions as to the approach of other traffic can sometimes be made by observing whether the road crossing your path is clear and open ; that is to say, where there is a crowd of people chatting amicably in the middle of the side turning or an old woman is hobbling slowly across to the other side, one may assume that nothing is coming.

Don't Judge by Appearances.

On the other hand, because such symptoms would appear to indicate that no cross traffic is approaching, it is most unwise definitely to conclude that you have a clear road. For one thing, the old woman in question may be deaf or have bad eyesight, so that she has not noticed another vehicle approaching, and is, in fact, in imminent danger of meeting with a mishap, while the group of people chatting in the middle of the roadway may be of the obstinate variety, and would rather that a motorcar took to the pavement to avoid them than disturb their conversation. Why when there are perfectly good pavements many feet wide on each side of the street the public should prefer to stand chatting in the middle of the road is a mystery, and will presumably remain a mystery for ever.

HOW TO DRIVE A CAR.

While on the subject of warning new drivers not to judge by appearances, it is as well to realize that a road-mender who appears to have reached middle age is not necessarily sensible, but, on the contrary, may be obstinate to the point of insanity. In the course of many years' driving under all sorts of conditions, the writer has come across obstinate men who would willingly (or it would appear so) be knocked down by a motorcar rather than the driver should have a free passage along the thoroughfare. It does not concern the individual that, in the effort to avoid him, the motorist may run into half a dozen cyclists or risk serious damage to some harmless and much more careful individual.

No reliance should be placed upon casual signals at blind crossings. The signaller may be well intentioned but may have failed to observe the approach of another car.

Don't Trust Other People.

A subject of equal importance to the new driver is the information which will be given to him by others. "Don't trust anyone for information which you cannot yourself verify and upon which safety depends" is the best motto to adopt. For example, many accidents have happened through a well-intentioned but unobservant pedestrian waving an "All-clear, come-on" signal at a blind cross-roads to a driver who forthwith proceeded without slackening speed, only to collide with a car approaching at right angles which the pedestrian had failed to see. Even when a policeman or an A.A. scout waves you on, it is as well to proceed cautiously until you can see for yourself that the way is clear ; it is always possible that some impetuous driver has not noticed the signal and is carrying on across your path.

Similarly with signals received from a driver ahead whom you wish to overtake ; a "wave-on" from him means that he is aware you are there and intends to let you pass, but it does emphatically not mean that you can rely upon a clear passage. Wait until you can see sufficient of the road ahead for yourself. Still more dangerous is it to take any notice of signals made by the passengers in motor coaches.

Another way in which you may get into difficulties through relying upon others is by following another car at close quarters, particularly if it be a saloon beyond which you cannot see. For example, the driver ahead may pull over to the right to pass a lorry in a narrow road, but you will be most unwise blindly to follow him ; a second later he may cut in front of the lorry, leaving you face to face with an approaching car which, until the last moment, was hidden from view.

Level-crossings.

The experienced motorist, with a naturally keen or carefully cultivated observation, often sees round corners by looking through hedges, bushes, trees, etc., and so is able to get an idea whether there is any traffic approaching or any such obstacle as a level-crossing.

Level-crossings are almost invariably signalled in this country by a danger sign, so a close lookout should be kept for these, although it is true that in England level-crossings on main roads are exceedingly rare, but on the Great North Road at one point there are three within a few miles. Generally, these are indicated at night by a red light, which remains there whether the gate be open or closed, and in any case forms a valuable warning, as even though the gate may be open, traversing a some-times very irregular and bumpy railway track might be the cause of an accident. On the gates themselves, how-ever, are generally small swivelling lights, which show green when the road is clear and red when it is obstructed.

In some parts of the country—Kent, for example—open railway crossings still exist with warning signs but no gates; although the rails in question may carry a very infrequent train service, it is, of course, particularly necessary to be cautious when approaching a crossing of this kind.

Dangerous Gates.

In wilder districts, such as parts of Yorkshire, Cum-berland, and the Devonshire moors, a close look-out should be kept for cattle gates, because these in remote districts are seldom provided with any lighting device at night. It is suggested that some such organization as the R.A.C. or A.A. might fix red reflectors of the cycle type to all such gates, so that they would show a red light reflected from headlamps. A useful example of this is situated on the Horsham road, coming towards London. Here, at a right-angle bend, where a large gateway confronts the motorist before he turns the cor-ner, several red reflectors are attached to the gate, while three are also screwed to the points of a triangular warn-ing sign erected by the Automobile Association 50 yards or so before the gate is reached.

An Arresting Effect.

These reflectors appear like so many red lamps, and immediately signal to the motorist an approaching dan-ger of some sort. Indeed, the effect is very similar to what is seen when the road is up and the broken-away portion surrounded with a rope festooned with red lan-terns. Such reflectors are now also becoming increas-ingly used for portable warning signs employed when re-surfacing and other work is being carried out.

Driving in Rain.

Much of the inconvenience of driving in rain is caused by the difficulty of seeing through the screen. Nowadays, windscreen wipers are sold in a truly amazing variety of shapes and sizes, while there are also numerous excellent preparations designed to supersede the paraffined rag, sliced apple or potato which were resorted to by motorists in earlier times to prevent raindrops accumulating on the screen.

With a clear screen one generally feels tolerably safe when driving, even in a heavy downpour. Nevertheless, greater vigilance is generally required, particularly in the case of a touring car where the side curtains impair the field of vision, so that it is necessary to move one's head fairly constantly whilst driving, especially when observing the left or right of the road. This is often, to some extent, obscured from view each side of the side curtain where it joins the windscreen. Again, the ordinary windscreen wiper clears only a small portion of the glass, and heavy rain on the remainder will result in its becoming almost opaque, so rendering it difficult for the driver to see towards the left of the road. Care is particularly necessary when negotiating a left-hand bend or corner in such circumstances.

Another reason for caution in wet weather is, of course, that on wet roads one has to allow a greater pulling-up space, owing to the likelihood of the car skidding on greasy surfaces. Generally speaking, it is wise to reduce the speed when traversing very wet or slippery roads, as this not only adds to the safety of the driver and passengers, but is less likely to cause annoyance to pedestrians by splashing their clothes with water from puddles through which the wheels may pass.

Skidding Purposely.

In a previous chapter considerable space was devoted to the question of correcting skids, and reference was at the same time made to the fact that it was possible to make a car skid, and that in some cases—chiefly, it is true, in emergencies—it might prove very useful if you

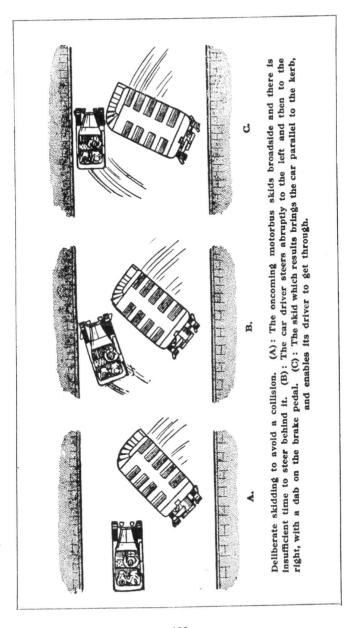

Deliberate skidding to avoid a collision. (A): The oncoming motorbus skids broadside and there is insufficient time to steer behind it. (B): The car driver steers abruptly to the left and then to the right, with a dab on the brake pedal. (C): The skid which results brings the car parallel to the kerb, and enables its driver to get through.

knew how to get out of a tight corner by making a well-executed skid.

Now it should be fully understood from the beginning that it is very far from good practice to skid round corners, as a matter of course, just for the fun of doing so. Any such skid tends to put a severe strain on the tyres, axles and transmission generally, and does not make for the longevity of the vehicle. At the same time, if you find a very greasy road, where there is no traffic, you can spend a very profitable hour or two deliberately causing skids and finding out what happens to the car.

It occasionally happens that you are faced with an emergency in which nothing but a well-executed skid can save you. For instance, supposing you are going along fairly well in the middle of the road and an approaching lorry were to skid its tail round to its right—i.e., across your path. This, of course, might happen quite suddenly, when you were only a few feet away. Now, if you simply steer to the left to get round the tail of the other vehicle, the rear part of your car might still catch the tailboard of the lorry, owing to the fact that there was only room for you to get through if your car kept absolutely straight and parallel to the kerb.

Avoiding an Accident.

In a case which came to the writer's knowledge, the driver of a small car was able to avoid a nasty accident in just such a case by skidding the back of his car round to the left, so that he brought the car, which was a second before in the middle of the road, right close to the kerb and parallel to it, and just managed to steer through where otherwise he must surely have been hit. What he did, of course, when he found that it was impossible for him to steer round the tail of the motorbus which skidded across his path, was to steer first to the left and then sharply to the right, at the same time giving a quick tap on the brake pedal. This, of course, would bring the tail of the car round to the left, when by steering to the left once more he was able to pursue a straight course.

HOW TO DRIVE A CAR.

Skidding Round Corners.

In the ordinary way, when driving well, one should never be faced with the problem of having to skid the car round a corner, as is done in road races. Nevertheless, it may happen that either when in a hurry or when driving at night with dim lamps so that a bend is not seen until too late, one may be faced with the problem of having to get round a corner when travelling too fast. Steering round in the ordinary way would very possibly cause the vehicle to overturn; or, at any rate, to slither into the bank and do some damage. The few remaining seconds before the bend is actually reached should be employed in decelerating by braking with the clutch in.

To turn left, for example, the car should be headed straight at the near-side corner of the kerb, and at the very moment when the front wheels become level with it, the wheels should be turned as if to steer round the corner and a firm touch given to the brake. This will cause the back of the car to swing round, and the very moment that the rear wheels are approximately in line with those in front you should accelerate.

Correcting a Skid by a Skid.

Correcting a skid by a skid is accomplished by making a "dive" to the off side of the road into which one has turned, waiting until the last moment before correcting the direction, so that one follows a straight line up the road. Actually, then, whether you are rounding a sharp corner or a mere bend (if faced with an emergency), where you can skid but not steer round, you should rely on the skid to turn, checking it immediately afterwards by violent acceleration. The subsequent procedure consists of steering against the skid in order to keep the car following the desired course.

It should be noted here that when four-wheel brakes are adjusted in such a way that as much (or more) of the braking force comes on the front wheels as on the rear wheels, which is, however, seldom the case, a car will be very reluctant to skid when braked. In such cases intentional skids of any magnitude can only be executed by using the hand brake in certain cases where this takes effect upon the rear wheels only.

The knowledge of how to skid and how to correct a skid forms part of the curriculum of the London bus driver, and it is said that the head instructors have become so skilful that they sometimes amuse themselves by taking a motorbus into the special greasy yard where skidding is practised, and skid the bus to and fro between rows of biscuit boxes or petrol tins without so much as knocking one out of place. To know how to skid is to possess always, as it were, a card up your sleeve which, produced at the last moment, may save your life or somebody else's.

The Art of Towing.

Should a breakdown occur you may find it necessary to telephone for assistance to a garage, and, if it is not found feasible to execute repairs on the spot, your car may have to be taken in tow. It is usually found rather disconcerting to drive under these conditions, so that a few hints will be helpful.

First, the rope should be attached to really substantial parts of the two cars concerned. The law requires that it shall not be more than 15 ft. in length, and that some warning device (such as a white handkerchief) should be tied to the rope between the vehicles. Before attempting to move off, the car in front should be driven forward very slowly until the rope is taut; then, if the driver engages the clutch very gently, the vehicles will get under way together without a jerk.

Although the driver of the leading vehicle should avoid excessive speed and sudden changes of speed, the man who is being towed must, nevertheless, be prepared to apply the brakes so as to avoid overrunning the towing vehicle. You must remember that on a downward gradient the car which is being towed, and is running freely in neutral, will tend to catch up with the vehicle ahead, so allowing the rope to become slack unless you apply the brakes in good time.

HOW TO DRIVE A CAR.

A slack rope trails on the ground and there is a risk that one of the wheels of the towed car may run over it ; then, when the leading vehicle goes ahead, the tightened rope may become wound round the front axle. For this and other reasons a system of horn signals should be agreed upon between the two drivers concerned, so that the man who is being towed can acquaint the leader if he is in difficulties. It is also advisable for the leading driver to keep an eye upon his charge by glancing occasionally into the driving mirror.

Towing a Caravan.

Caravanning has become very popular with motorists, and, provided that some discretion is exercised as to the touring ground selected, it is possible to tow a van with quite a small car. The pull required is, however, considerable, so that a proper rig should be attached to the back of the car to take the bar by which the caravan is drawn along.

So far as legal requirements are concerned, the speed limit with a caravan or trailer of any type is 30 m.p.h., and this should not be exceeded. Furthermore, a number plate must be carried at the rear end of the van (bearing the same registration as the car), and must be illuminated at night with a tail lamp of the usual type showing red to the rear. In many cases special arrangements for insurance must also be made.

There is no need to fear difficulties in driving a car with a caravan attached. Just a little more care and judgment are required in traffic and when negotiating sharp bends, but the revision in driving methods is really only slight. One must, of course, make allowance for the fact that the car will be more sluggish, this and the length of the van making it essential to exercise special care when overtaking other vehicles. Other points to remember are that the van may be a little wider than the car, that its wheels may not follow exactly the same track on a bend, and that humped bridges should not be taken at too high a speed.

HOW TO DRIVE A CAR.

The way in which the car will handle depends partly upon how the trailer is loaded. The usual two-wheeled caravan is so designed as to be slightly nose-heavy, and, for the best results, all the spare luggage should be placed at the forward end, thus increasing the downward force on the tow bar.

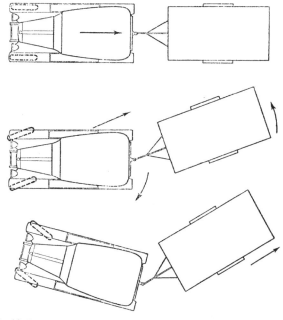

Backing a caravan : To steer towards the off side, the front wheels must first be deflected to the left, so swinging the tail of the car in the direction shown. Then, when the caravan has taken up an angular position, the steering wheels can be deflected in the opposite direction.

The tow bar is always fitted with an automatic device which applies brakes to the caravan wheels when the trailer commences to overrun the car. Consequently, so soon as the caravan is reversed by the car, this brake comes into operation. It is, therefore, essential to peg up the thrust bar, so that the brakes do not function, before attempting to reverse. When the caravan has been placed in position, release the peg from the brake gear so that it is free to function again.

When practising backing, do not be discouraged if the trailer sets itself in the opposite direction to that in which one desires to proceed. This is what will happen if the car is steered in the ordinary way. What you must do is to steer in the way shown in the accompanying sketches. That is, at the outset lock the wheels over directly in the opposite way to that employed when the car is being normally backed.

If the tail of the car in the ordinary way were to be swung to the right the front wheels would be locked over that way ; with the caravan in tow, or rather being pushed, to direct it to the right, the front wheels of the car must be locked over to the left so as to swing the tail of the car in that direction. This has the effect of locking over the trailer to the right, in which direction it can then be pushed. So soon as the required angle has been reached, lock the steering over in the opposite direction and reverse in the ordinary way.

There may be certain circumstances in which it is necessary to unhitch the car from the trailer when it has been placed in the required position, and man-handle it before hitching up again to give it a direct push back. This two-stage operation might have to be used, for example, to get through an awkward gateway.

Driving in Fog.

We will conclude this chapter by a few notes upon driving a car in fog, the one weather condition (apart from exceptionally heavy snow) which may make the modern car undrivable. Of course, if the fog is extremely thick and your nerve gets "rattled," the only thing to do is give up. However, certain methods can be adopted which will enable you to carry on in circumstances that would otherwise make driving very dangerous.

First of all, do not use the headlamps, even in a fairly light mist, unless you have a dipping mechanism ; a straight-ahead beam of white light is reflected back from the fog, producing the effect of an impenetrable wall. Yellow covers, lamp screens and tinted bulbs can be obtained which colour the beams and ease driving conditions considerably, particularly if the beams can be dipped and deflected to the left, as is now possible with many of the headlamp-control mechanisms available.

A lamp mounted on a dumbiron and deflected as shown is a great help when driving in a really thick fog.

In a really thick fog the aim should be to get illumination which will show up the edge of the road near to the car, which must be used as a guide by the driver. He must also endeavour to keep an eye ahead, as it were, to avoid running into an obstacle. Very useful types of spotlight can be obtained which can be fitted to a bracket on the near-side running board, or the front dumbiron, for use in fog. Most drivers also find it easier to make their way in safety with the windscreen open.

HOW TO DRIVE A CAR.

In foggy weather, do not put on too much speed in a "clear patch," as you may run into a further misty section of road with disconcerting suddenness. In winter this is particularly dangerous, as the fog may be accompanied by a frozen film of moisture over the road surface, so that applying the brakes will lead to a skid : and a skid on ice when fog makes it impossible to see is a most unpleasant and dangerous experience.

CHAPTER VIII.

Some Finer Points in Driving. Courtesy and Consideration for Others. Effects of Sudden Tyre Deflation. Handling the Controls.

The first requisite for all motorists is that of coolness, and coupled with this should invariably run a strong undercurrent of gentlemanly behaviour. Luckily the road-hog is in a distinct minority in the various classes of motoring, but nevertheless there is still a number of motorists who are not quite so considerate in their driving principles and manners as one would wish to see them; some from selfishness and some from ignorance.

It is almost impossible to define any series of specific instances to make the point more lucid, but the whole basis of good road manners turns on the pivot of considerateness. This word should have an all-embracing width of meaning, not only to other road users as such and to humanity, but even to mere animal life of the small order, which one meets ever and anon in the course of one's travels.

Special Cases to be Considered.

There are odd occasions which occur when it would be wrong for a motorist to pay attention to such things if it should be a case where his own safety and that of the occupants of the car, or other people's safety on the road, would really be endangered.

For instance, when one is travelling at a good speed on a greasy road or in a confined space and a dog or other animal suddenly runs in front of the car and nothing but a violent application of the brake could avoid hitting it, and it is a foregone conclusion that such brake application must carry in its wake a bad or dangerous skid, then one is reluctantly compelled to let the animal in question take care of itself as best it can. However, these circumstances are certainly rather the exception than the rule, and in all other cases due consideration should be given to all animal life.

Another failing to which we are all more or less likely to fall victims is the one of assuming that because the horn has been sounded, the person for whom the warning has been given is aware of the fact that such is the case. It may be, perchance, that a man is leading a heavy dray, and that his hearing is not of the best, or that he may even be deaf. If, therefore, he does not move quite so fast as one would wish, do not for that reason abuse him, as it is no crime to be deaf, and the law does not as yet place any restriction on the clatter which a horse-drawn vehicle may make. For similar reasons the driver of a heavy lorry may appear loth to draw to the near side in order to allow you to overtake ; do not jump to the conclusion that he is deliberately obstructing you, and signify your disapproval by " cutting-in" viciously when at last you get a chance to overtake.

The Philosophic Mind.

No. The driver of a car should always carry with him, as his stock-in-trade, a large fund of philosophy, and draw on it copiously for each such instance which he encounters.

It must be remembered that the balance in ordinary humanity between perfection and imperfection is largely in favour of the latter quality, and many people will always be ignorant, or even stupid, in their behaviour on the road. It will be found far more enjoyable, and considerably more beneficial in all such cases where one may even have a just cause for annoyance, to draw on one's fund of philosophy and recognize that such things must be, treating the incident in question with good humour or a smile of indulgence, as one may feel inclined.

HOW TO DRIVE A CAR.

Again, do not make the common mistake of putting on speed when you notice that a faster car is about to overtake you ; there is no disgrace in being passed, and it is foolish to travel faster than you really wish just to keep some inoffensive individual behind.

Mud Splashing.

When driving on wet roads, one should always keep an eye on the possibilities of splashing pedestrians when passing them. A car driven over a large puddle at a good speed will splash mud and water out sideways for a very considerable distance ; in fact, to a far greater extent than most people imagine.

A considerate driver when out under such road conditions always keeps a wary eye for large puddles in his path, so that, if reasonably possible, he will miss them with his near-side wheels and thus avoid the possibility of splashing people on the path.

The Freemasonry of the Road.

It is rather to be feared that the one-time generally existing freemasonry of the road is not practised much in the motor world nowadays.

Whenever one chances to meet a fellow-motorist who is in difficulties on the roadside, it is certainly a most commendable proceeding to slow down and ask if one can be of any assistance. It may be the smallest of minor troubles which is holding him up, and that one can with but very little inconvenience to oneself assist the fellow-motorist in distress.

For instance, one may run out of petrol, and a gallon of this at any time valuable spirit may be of exceptionally great value to a stranded motorist who is in a hurry to get on. It may be the stranded one wants a plug, or the loan of a tyre pump, or a valve for a tube, or some other insignificant detail which one could supply (and, of course, if of any value accept payment for) with but very little inconvenience. Then, again, it may be that the stranded motorist is held up by some very simple little trouble which a few words of advice from a more experienced driver may quickly rectify.

Offering Assistance.

The writer invariably makes a point of slowing down and asking if assistance is required whenever he meets a fellow-motorist—of any classification whatsoever—in a state of distress at the roadside. There might, of course, be odd occasions when one could not possibly spare the time, or where the loneliness of a road at night might make it seem unwise to stop, but these are rare exceptions.

It is to be hoped, then, that this spirit of freemasonry may revive, and those motorists not disposed to help others in such cases should remember that on some occasion they may be similarly stranded, when time is a matter of considerably more than the average importance, and that then they would certainly be the first to think they were ill-treated if they could not obtain some simple roadside assistance from passing fellow-motorists.

Some General Advice.

Never allow yourself to become addicted to the bad practice of showing off. For instance, there is nothing particularly clever in causing the rear wheels to spin or skid round at a great speed when starting away. Neither is there anything particularly clever in driving up to a traffic block or other necessary stoppage at a high speed and then jamming on the brakes so as to effect a spectacular stop. Any credit there is rests with the machine and its maker and not with the driver. Similarly, there is no credit whatsoever in turning round in the road in a half-circle at such a speed as nearly to force the front tyre off its rim. Such practices to the expert driver or mechanically minded person are amongst the worst sins of the mechanical world. Reversing with great rapidity is also a reprehensible practice which often leads to damage or even accidents.

Make a habit of giving a due measure of importance to cross-roads, even although they may be of an insignificant character. Similarly, try to cultivate a calm philosophy when finding another car faster than your own, and do not let the fact prove annoying that a car passes which one happens to know is about the same power as one's own machine. Anything in the nature of racing on the road is to be deprecated, as it tends to kill that most desirable characteristic, sangfroid, and excitement will perhaps lead one or both of the parties concerned into taking undue risks with their own cars or with the safety of other users of the highway.

If inclined for speed work, choose the right sort of road for it. Never go fast down a steep hill, or, for that matter, down any hill, particularly on a road you have not traversed before ; the extra braking effort necessary to stop the car in case of emergency is enormous and is rarely understood.

Never take corners at too great a speed. Remember that it is against the laws of mechanics, and that one corner taken at an excessive speed will put more strain on the front-wheel bearings and steering gear than a very considerable amount of straightforward running.

Always endeavour to use the brakes as little as possible. The more skilful the driver the less frequently does he employ violent braking effect.

Risks of Close-up Driving.

In traffic do not follow too closely in the wake of a tram, bus, or other mechanically propelled vehicle, as there is nothing particularly clever in running, as so many taxi drivers do, with the mudguard or lamps only a foot from the rear of the preceding vehicle, and it only brings into play a considerable amount of excessive braking. Some people are wont to express the opinion that, because so-and-so drives like this, he is a skilful driver and possessed of sound judgment. Such an opinion is entirely erroneous and such conduct is nothing more or less than rank bad driving. In the case of necessity it is well to be able to judge things by a small margin, but when there is no necessity it is only foolish.

In the case of an accident, whether one is concerned in it or not, humanity demands that the driver should proffer assistance.

HOW TO DRIVE A CAR.

Talking when Driving.

The question of to what extent the driver of a car should converse with his passengers is an important one, but much depends upon the temperament of the individual. Most people find that they can drive and take a reasonable interest in light conversation at the same time, but on no account should the driver let his eyes or attention stray from the road. In the second or so during which he turns his head some emergency may arise to demand his immediate attention, and the few instants that may elapse before he turns to the road again may be fatal to the avoidance of an accident. Another common cause of trouble is the lack of concentration on the road of a driver who is not sure of his route and is gazing around at a signpost or is looking for the name of a street. Many cars are now being fitted with radio, and here, again, the driver must exercise concentration to avoid distraction from the road.

Do not make too great a use of the horn, especially if it is of the loud-toned variety. It is bad taste, and one should remember that everyone has an equal right to the proper use of the roads.

Effects of Tyre Deflation.

If the steering seems suddenly to pull to one side, it is usually an indication that one of the tyres is becoming deflated. If the pull is a heavy one to the left, it is probably the near-side front tyre ; if to the right, the off side. If it has a tendency to pull first one way and then the other, it will probably be found to be one of the rear tyres.

If landed with a punctured tyre and no spare tyre and wheel or means for repairing it, and there is a garage, say, some few miles along the road, the car can be driven very gently and as slowly as it can run on the top gear (not exceeding five miles an hour), and it is possible to get to such garage without seriously damaging either the tube or the cover: the writer has done it many a time and oft. If it is the near-side front tyre which is causing such trouble, get the front passenger into the back on the right-hand side of the car.   If a rear tyre and there are passengers in the back, get them, so far as possible, to sit on the opposite side of the car.

The sudden deflation of an off-side front tyre will precipitate a swerve to the right unless the driver is maintaining a firm grip on the wheel.

Investigate a Noise at Once.

If an unaccustomed noise develops, it should be investigated without delay.   A squeak which cannot be easily traced is often due to one of the universal joints.   Do not forget that front wheels occasionally require some lubricant, and if ever a car appears to run stiffly, an examination should at once be undertaken to find, first of all, whether there is anything wrong with the engine by cranking it in order to ascertain whether it will turn freely.   If it is all right, then feel each brake drum in turn, as a binding brake will set up great resistance and cause the drum to become very hot.

HOW TO DRIVE A CAR.

Occasionally have a look in the radiator, and replenish it; do not fill it to the top, but only to within about an inch of the overflow pipe. It must be remembered that the water has to expand, and if by any chance the overflow pipe should have become partially blocked with dirt or through other means, and the heating of the water in the radiator is accomplished at a great speed, sufficient pressure may be generated by its expansion to cause a leak in that delicate fitment.

Carry Spare Oil.

Spare lubricating oil should always be carried on long runs, and with regard to the question of lubrication always remember that a little oil supplied frequently is very much better than waiting until a portion of the machinery makes it manifest that it wants some more lubrication and then giving it a good dose. Charts are usually supplied with cars which show how often each bearing should receive attention from the grease gun or oil can.

Watch the Oil in the Sump.

So far as the engine is concerned, always keep an eye on it from the lubrication point of view, acting according to the instructions of the makers. A well-made engine of 12 h.p. or 15 h.p. should do something in the neighbourhood of 1,000 miles to 1,500 miles to a gallon of oil; some cars do a good deal more. Check the level periodically by means of the device provided on the crankcase and keep an eye on the pressure gauge, which will become unsteady when the level is low. If touring in a very hilly country where many hills have to be encountered on low gears, it is a good plan to put in a little fresh oil, whether it is time for it or not. Similarly, if one is doing 250 miles per week, it is preferable to put in a quart of oil each week than a gallon at the end of the month. Never run any risks with regard to the amount of oil in the engine, as failure of the lubrication system can result in very extensive damage to the bearings and the pistons. Every 1,000 miles to 2,000 miles or so (according to the makers' instructions) some fresh lubricant should be added to the gearbox, and similarly the lubricant in the rear-axle casing should be brought up to its proper level on such occasions.

A Golden Rule.

A golden rule for safe driving is as follows:—*Never under any conditions whatsoever drive at a speed in excess of that at which a sufficient distance of clear road can be actually seen ahead in which comfortably to stop by the application of the brakes.* A whole book could be written on the subject of dangerous situations, but, to the writer's mind, it really seems not worth while. A hundred examples might be given, and it would be the hundred-and-first which the reader might come against. If this one golden rule is invariably adhered to the occasion when one will be involved in an accident through one's own fault is a very remote possibility. To instance one special case where this advice is important, the well-known hump-backed bridge may be quoted, and one should declutch when sufficiently near the top of this to know that the momentum of the car will carry it over the brow, and it should only be surmounted at such a speed that, if necessary, one can stop in a few yards. Of all rules for careful driving, the one italicized above is the mainspring. If it is honestly adhered to one need not really say anything much beyond that, so far as the question of speed is concerned. It is an automatic governor for the safety and well-being of oneself, one's car, and all other road users.

Minor Driving Refinements.

When you have had several months' driving experience your attention will no longer be taken up to quite the same extent with the anxiety as to whether or no you will succeed in making a quiet gear change, or whether that motor lorry or horsed vehicle is going to pull out suddenly in front of you. You can then settle down to drive without effort and will be able to devote a little more attention to refinements, from a mechanical point of view, of handling a car.

HOW TO DRIVE A CAR.

Perhaps all this time you have been driving without touching the ignition control (if one is fitted to your car), or maybe you have been using it in accordance with the makers' instructions in their handbook, without really knowing why you should do so. You will probably have found out, however, that if you move it too far in the "advance" direction the engine will emit a metallic knocking sound known as "pinking," while if you move it too far back you will get less power from the engine. Perhaps the movement of the ignition lever has very little effect; this depends on the type of power unit.

Better Work with Correct Ignition Setting.

In any case, generally speaking, the engine will run more efficiently if the ignition is set correctly for the conditions under which it is working. For instance, when doing a speed effort on the level, it is desirable to go on advancing the ignition until the maximum speed on a given throttle opening has been reached. On the other hand, when accelerating on top gear, when climbing a steep hill slowly, or when starting, it is better to retard the ignition, subsequently advancing it as the engine speed increases.

When the car has magneto ignition, the advance and retard lever generally has less effect than where battery ignition is employed, chiefly because with most magnetos the best spark occurs when the ignition is fully advanced, whereas with battery and coil the spark is equally effective at any engine speed and whether it is advanced or retarded.

Dangers of Over-advance.

Driving with the ignition too far advanced is severe on the bearings and tends to cause vibration and uneven running; because, although when travelling fast the spark is set to occur before the piston reaches dead centre, so that the mixture is properly burning and expanding to its maximum extent just as top dead centre is reached, it should be borne in mind that with the mixture igniting some time before the piston has reached the top of its stroke a heavy blow is given to it in the opposite direction to that in which it should be moving—that is, a blow tending momentarily to reverse the engine.

On the other hand, driving with the ignition too far retarded, besides giving less power owing to the fact that the mixture is not being ignited at the most suitable

On cars not fitted with automatic ignition timing an improved performance can be obtained by an intelligent use of the advance-retard lever.

moment for forcing down the pistons, causes the engine to get unduly hot because the mixture continues to burn through a larger proportion of the down stroke and more heat is lost to the jackets.

Automatic Advance.

On some cars, of course, an automatic advance is fitted, which takes the responsibility for manipulating the ignition lever out of the hands of the driver. On other cars the ignition is fixed in the position deemed to be the most efficient by the makers.

On certain cars, especially those fitted with battery ignition, an excellent test of the effect of advancing or retarding the ignition can be made if the control lever is moved backwards and forwards gently when the car is running slowly. It will then be found, especially on low-compression engines, that it has quite an appreciable effect on the speed of the vehicle, the car gradually slowing down as the ignition is retarded.

The small high-efficiency engine gives much better service if intelligent use is made of the ignition control, as the necessarily high compression is apt to cause "pinking"—especially when running on undiluted petrol. The ignition should, in any case, be retarded when starting an engine. With hand cranking, this reduces the risk of a kick back; with a starter motor the drive is safeguarded from damage for the same reason.

CHAPTER IX.

Accidents—Avoidable and Unavoidable. What to Do if Involved in One.

To some people the very word "accident" is enough to cause a shudder. They mention the word in hushed voices as if it must of necessity be one resulting in fatal injuries to some unfortunate person; yet perhaps 75 per cent. of mishaps that the insurance people would class under this heading amount to nothing more than scratched or buckled wings or damaged headlamps.

For instance, if you are driving along the road on a wet, slippery day, and a car in front of you suddenly executes an unexpected skid so that, unable to pull up, you drive into it, you are involved in an accident. A crowd collects, the inevitable policeman arrives with his notebook, and you immediately find yourself for the moment as great a celebrity as if you had been involved in something infinitely more serious.

Two Types of Accident.

There are really two types of accident—the avoidable and the unavoidable. If you drive carefully, possess a reasonable degree of road sense, and generally obey the written and unwritten rules of the road, you will seldom be involved in one of the former type, but among the latter are such causes as unintentional skids by other road users, carelessness, casual or criminal, on the part of drivers of other cars, or the heedless dashing out of a child or animal into the middle of the highway.

In every case it is important to keep cool; also it is desirable that preliminary explanations, at any rate, should come only from the driver. A sensible passenger, in the event of an accident, will generally keep his or her head and silently await developments, but many

are those who, perhaps rendered nervous by fairly fast
travelling, declare excitedly, just as the policeman steps
to your side, that they "knew you were going too fast,"
or "I had a feeling that something horrible was going
to happen."

About "Sounding the Horn."

You should realize with what importance the police
are apt to regard the sounding of the horn. In a previous chapter, when to sound a warning device was fully
discussed, and it was decided that in certain conditions
it was rather more dangerous to sound the hooter than
not to do so. At the same time, whenever a pedestrian
has had the misfortune to be knocked down, or two
vehicles, one of them a car, have met at the cross-roads,
the first question asked by the policeman is almost invariably, "Did you sound your horn?" Therefore,
hooting, at cross-roads at any rate, is practically a duty.
The cooler you can keep the better, for often an otherwise calm individual will, in the excitement of the
moment, make statements which he would give much to
recall.

Obtain Witnesses.

In any sort of accident you should stop at once and
have all essential measurements taken, and immediately,
before those to whom a motor smash does not prove an
irresistible "draw" have had time to melt away, you
should obtain the names and addresses of all available
witnesses. Very often the most level-headed and perhaps the most impartial spectators of a motor mishap
carry on calmly with their business or pleasure, while
anti-motoring fanatics gather round. Generally speaking, the most favourable witnesses are the first to go,
hostile people who have nothing to do being, for the
most part, those who stay on. In the event of minor
collisions involving damaged lamps or wings, the
quickest method of dealing with the matter is generally
for the owners or drivers of the two cars to exchange
cards, subsequently communicating to their respective
insurance companies details of the occurrence.

On the other hand, if any such encounter results in injury to a human being, all possible succour should first be given to the injured individual. At the same time, if you keep a clear head, you will probably realize that where you have come to an abrupt stop, often in the middle of the highway, is likely to cause congestion and obstruction to other traffic, so after having pointed out the position in which you drew up to any policeman or responsible person present, you would do well to pull your car well into the side of the road, and generally

A crowd is apt to gather quickly after even the mildest of mishaps.

make the fact that a mishap has occurred inconspicuous.

If anything has happened of an untoward nature when you are at the wheel, the policeman will, on his arrival, ask to see your driving licence and insurance certificate, and will extract certain particulars therefrom. He will also take the number of the car and your statement of the affair, together with any remarks from individual spectators.

Very often, after the policeman has written pages of notes, you will hear nothing more of the occurrence. Sometimes you may get a claim for real or imaginary injuries from the third party, but the best thing to do in such a case is to forward the letter immediately to your insurance company.

HOW TO DRIVE A CAR.

Never Offer Money.

If you have been so unfortunate as to knock down someone, you should never in any circumstance make an offer of money. The temptation may be strong to do so, when you find that some poor old man or woman has carelessly stepped from behind the tram immediately in your path and thus got knocked down, but, unfortunately, the law regards any such demonstration of sympathy as the giving of money as a direct admission that you were in the wrong. The law argues thus, "Why should anybody in their right senses want to pay for damage caused by somebody else?"

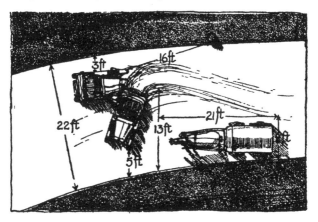

A rough sketch of this kind can be made to show essential measurements when an accident has occurred.

The Etiquette of the Road.

Human nature is so constituted that half the hostility existing between one class and another in this world is due to envy. However one may consider the question of why, among a certain class of people, motorists are disliked, one invariably comes to the conclusion that one of the most primitive of human emotions plays an important part. If the average person who cannot afford a car had no use for one, he would, provided that automobiles did not become a nuisance, merely tolerate the presence of car drivers on the road, regarding them perhaps as eccentric cranks who took pleasure in some silly and profitless pastime.

As it is, however, the man tramping home through the rain sees another drive swiftly past in a comfortable saloon, and immediately the forces of envy get to work. He thinks to himself, "Why should he get home in ten minutes, keeping quite dry and warm, while I trudge through the rain for three-quarters of an hour every night after my day's work is done?" And on holidays, too, when he sees one car load after another speeding out of town and realizes that in 20 minutes—half an hour perhaps at most—they can be in the free and open country, whereas if he would leave the wilderness of brick and mortar wherein he is forced to have his being, he must needs "queue up" for a tram or omnibus to spend half a day getting to and from the green fields, the woods and the sunshine for which his nature craves.

Verily, even the most humble possessor of a self-propelled vehicle on two, three or four wheels is much to be envied. He holds the key to the open country, to fresh air, and has the means of comfortable, effortless travel from home to work and back again.

The Motorist a Newcomer.

Also, the motorist is a comparative newcomer to our roads. Thousands of years before him, first over untrodden land and later along tracks which became gradually more and more marked, came travellers on foot, heavy burdens bowing their shoulders, pack-horses, mules, preceded by one knows not what queer prehistoric beasts of burden. One pictures the web-footed horses which scientists tell us were the progenitors of the magnificent animals of to-day, flopping through marshy lowlands, and, perhaps thousands of years later, with harder hoofs, picking their stumbling way along heights and ridgeways, which were the earliest highways of men, for in those days unknown terrors, wild beasts and robbers lurked in the densely wooded valleys of Wiltshire and Surrey. Hence, only on the bare ridges, like the Hog's Back, near Guildford, and round by Newlands Corner and the chain of downs reaching ultimately to the coast, was there any security to the hardened traveller of olden times.

The motorcar, then, is in reality a usurper, although so useful it is that within the last decade the winding roads along which stage coaches used to rumble are giving way to broad, straight highways ; hilltops are being levelled and valleys filled up in order to make way for the new traffic which is revolutionizing the world. Nevertheless, it is not much more than a quarter of a century since horse traction preponderated, and thus a very great number of people not only in this country, but in every part of the world, have not changed their thoughts as swiftly as motor transport has altered tra-velling ; so it behoves the motorist to drive always with such consideration that proves that he realizes that, at any rate for a generation, he is only tolerated on the roads.

Consideration.

After all, apart from the question of envy which we have already discussed, and which, childish though it may seem, is too much ingrained in human nature to be altogether discounted, the motorist does undoubtedly make a nuisance of himself. True, the considerate driver of a car does not take pleasure in driving at break-neck pace through villages in the small hours of the morning with headlights blazing and Klaxon wildly hooting—a practice which, alas! seems to be beloved of our friends across the Channel—but in the ordinary way of driving, a motorist can become a real nuisance when, secure in his all-weather vehicle, he splashes wet mud on to the garments of possibly less-fortunate pedestrians. He also, although to a much less extent than was formerly the case, raises dust. At night, in order to see where he is going, he often dazzles others with his lamps. Also he transforms what were once pretty, quiet portions of the King's highway, used perhaps seldom over their entire length, into a rushing stream of more or less noisy vehicles, wherefore pedestrians and cyclists prefer to take to the narrower byways which the motorist does not so much frequent.

Then in ordinary driving, whether in towns or on the open road, too much consideration can hardly be given to the aged or infirm. Most decent-minded motorists will stop, even if it means momentarily holding up the traffic behind them, while a crippled man or woman hobbles across the highway. They will show the same consideration to an old or obviously nervous man or woman. It costs very little either in time or in average speed.

Bad Manners—Not Clever.

To squeeze between a woman or man on crutches and another vehicle is not so much an exhibition of good driving as one of bad manners, and by reducing his speed or coming to a complete standstill and compelling those behind him to do the same, the motorist is preventing any possible example of that rare, but much-hated, species, the "road hog," from passing on where he has stopped.

Motor Beggars; and Giving "Lifts" on the Road.

It is quite possible to overdo road courtesy. For instance, if one were to stop and ask every pedestrian on the road if he or she would like a lift, one would never get anywhere. Also, in many cases, it turns out that someone so addressed is walking for their pleasure and does not want a lift at all.

On the other hand, there are only too many of what one might term motor beggars on the road who make a practice of the "art." An individual stands at the roadside, seeing a car approaching, perhaps fast, and extends his hand as a signal for the driver to stop. The motorist pulls up to see what is the matter. The man asks for a lift, which is generally immediately offered, to some place farther along the road, and the worthless vagabond then proceeds to take advantage of his position beside the motorist (who, for some obscure reason, he invariably imagines to be rich, regardless of whether the man may be a poorly paid employee driving someone else's car) to try first to excite sympathy, and then extract money from the driver who has already been kind enough to help him on his way.

Driver Liable for Passenger's Injuries.

Should the driver unfortunately meet with an accident and this casual passenger be injured, the driver of the car is himself liable for any claims the passenger might make against him. That in itself is enough to discourage one

Some discretion is desirable as to the kind of person to whom one may give a lift.

from giving lifts to strangers. On the other hand, when effecting a long journey alone, any company is sometimes more pleasant than none.

Apart from the types of accident we have so far discussed in this chapter, dangers may arise in connection with the car itself. Failure of the brakes has been mentioned earlier ; another possible cause of trouble is the sudden bursting of a tyre when the car is travelling fast. The first thought of the novice is to apply the brakes, but this is the worst thing to do, as the retarding force so placed on the wheel may easily cause the cover to be dragged off the rim. The car should simply be allowed to come to rest of itself (if a sufficient length of clear road be available), and should be kept to a straight course so far as may be practicable. If it is a front tyre that fails, a swerve will follow, which must be corrected immediately by exerting full strength on the wheel.

In the Event of a Fire.

Luckily, fires are very rare in the case of cars on the road ; but, nevertheless, the driver should know what to do. A "pop back" through the carburetter will occasionally be sufficiently violent to ignite the petrol in the float chamber, and the best antidote is to stop the car, turn off the petrol, and allow the engine to continue running until it exhausts the supply in the float chamber, which will not take long if the throttle be opened to make the engine race. A collection of oil or grease in the undershield has been known to become ignited, and here sand or earth should be thrown on the flames—not water ; or, better still, a fire extinguisher brought into action. A smell of burning may be traceable simply to a binding brake, slipping clutch, or faulty wiring, but should, of course, be investigated at once.

Some Common Mistakes.

Both petrol and benzole being of a highly inflammable character, one should always guard against smoking when filling a tank, as well as in the garage itself. Smoking, per se, is, in the writer's opinion, so far removed from the possibility of causing an accident that it can be discounted from the realms of practical politics ; but, nevertheless, the advice should be adhered to strictly on account of the ever-present possibility of striking a match to light a cigarette or cigar, which is potentially risky.

It is not the glow of the cigarette, cigar, or pipe which is so dangerous ; but if there is any vapour about or any of the spirit spilt anywhere, then the situation may be entirely changed into one of great danger by striking a match to light up again.

HOW TO DRIVE A CAR.

Another point to remember is that when filling up with spirit, on an odd occasion a garage hand (occasionally one is guilty of the negligence oneself) may overfill the tank and cause a considerable quantity of the spirit to be spilt. If the tank is in the dashboard a large proportion of this may find its way under the bonnet and under the floorboards into the precincts of the engine. If the tank is in the rear, a good deal may be in the neighbourhood of the exhaust pipe. In either case the engine should not be started up, more especially in an enclosed space, until such time as that spirit has entirely evaporated.

Causes of Petrol Fires.

With the dashboard tank, a little of the spirit getting into the distributor of the magneto may be ignited by a spark or there may be a short circuit somewhere. In the other case a backfire or a pop-back in the carburetter may cause a flame at the end of the exhaust pipe. In such an event, therefore, there is a distinct danger of causing a fire, and it should invariably be guarded against by mopping up the petrol with a piece of rag and waiting until the spirit has evaporated.

In this connection, it is quite sound advice to suggest that one should always keep an eye on all petrol connections; see that the unions on the pipes have not developed a leak. Similarly, that the carburetter has not contracted a habit of flooding, or that the tank itself has not sprung a leak. All these conditions present a distinct element of danger, and should be rectified at the earliest possible moment. Finally, there is the electrical equipment to consider; in course of time the insulation may become frayed, with the result that a short circuit may occur quite suddenly, accompanied by the unmistakable smell of burning rubber. This may necessitate getting at the accumulators to remove the positive lead.

Carry a Fire Extinguisher.

It is a wise precaution to carry one of the well-proved fire extinguishers specially made for car use. One of these small devices is particularly effective against a petrol fire, whereas water is useless.

CHAPTER X.

Economical Driving.

When one reads that a car of a certain make has recorded a certain petrol consumption in an authentic trial, and then compares the figure obtained with that which is usually put up by the private owner, it is often somewhat bewildering to know exactly how the result was reached. In the first place, of course, the car when on test was handled by a driver who, knowing that his aim and object was to use as little petrol as possible, used all the various artifices that can be employed in the attainment of a low fuel consumption. If the average owner-driver handled his car in a like manner, it must be admitted that he would obtain very little pleasure out of motoring. Speed, for example, has a marked effect; many cars use 50 per cent. more fuel when driven at 50 m.p.h. than when cruising at a gentle 25 m.p.h.

Saving Petrol.

Nevertheless, by the employment of a little care and the assimilation of certain habits many gallons of fuel could be saved in the course of a year's running without seriously minimizing the enjoyment one obtains from motoring.

A great many drivers use almost as much petrol when the car is descending a hill as they use when it is pulling normally on the level. There is a distinct art in coasting. It must be understood that the usual type of throttle is set so that it does not close entirely when the foot is taken off the accelerator pedal, but comes back to what is known as the slow-running position.

In these circumstances the whole of the suction of the engine is directed on the pilot jet, which is set to deliver a normally strong mixture when the engine is turning over slowly. Thus, when the engine is running fast—as is the case when the car is travelling downhill—a very strong suction is exerted on the pilot or slow-running jet, the result being that a rich mixture is drawn into the engine. Although this forms in the cylinders a mixture which may fire, it is, nevertheless, wholly wasted, for it performs no useful purpose. When travelling downhill, therefore, the driver can adopt alternative practices—one is to put the clutch out and to keep it out, so that the engine is disconnected from the road wheels, and the other is to place the gears in neutral, allowing the clutch to be normally engaged.

Effect on the Clutch.

Both these methods have drawbacks. If the clutch is continually kept out, it is more than probable that all the lubricant will be taken off the surfaces of the clutch withdrawal mechanism, which will soon become worn and noisy. It is not designed to withstand prolonged usage of this kind.

If the gears are put in neutral it means that the driver cannot rely on his engine for use as a brake in case of emergency, and, in point of fact, it often gives rise to a feeling of insecurity to know that the engine is in " free," although this method can, of course, usefully be employed on a hill that is long and straight, has no side turnings, and with the characteristics of which the driver is well acquainted. Everyone should make himself fully practised in the art of re-engaging gear when a car is coasting, as described earlier in this book.

Switching Off the Ignition.

A question that has often been asked is, " Should the ignition be switched off when descending a hill, the engine being left in connection with the transmission—that is to say, both the clutch and the gears being engaged? " On some cars the ignition can be switched off to advantage; on the majority it cannot. If the ignition is switched off, the throttle should not be left closed, for the reason that when the engine is running at a fair rate of revolutions with the throttle nearly shut, very little gas can get from the carburetter to the induction passages and thence to the cylinder head, so that what is practically a vacuum is formed inside the cylinders, which immediately has the effect of causing oil from the crankcase to be more readily drawn up past the pistons than would otherwise be the case, and this oil, accumulating in the cylinder head, may find its way on to the points of the sparking plugs and on to the valve seating.

Therefore, if the ignition is switched off, the throttle should be kept open, i.e., the accelerator pedal be fully depressed. On most cars, however, this causes banging in the silencer when the ignition is once again switched on, owing to the unburnt mixture which has accumulated there. This is certainly annoying and may damage the silencer, while the method does not result in any great economy.

The Extra-air Valve.

The only really economical method of coasting downhill is to employ an extra-air valve. These useful accessories can now be bought at a fairly low price, and they certainly result in marked economy, for, without switching off the ignition, they can be opened so soon as the car shows an ability to run downhill without the power of the engine, and not only do they economize petrol by taking the suction off the pilot jet in the carburetter, but, additionally, they scavenge the engine by providing it with a supply of cool, clean air, which sweeps through its interior parts and is generally beneficial.

On cars that are fitted with mixture-controlling devices the driver should, of course, always see that these are set to full weak when coasting down a hill.

The motto for the driver who wishes to motor as economically as possible should be: "Never do anything suddenly." Nothing uses petrol quicker than rapid acceleration, and, although this may be pleasingly spectacular, it is extremely wasteful. To accelerate a car quickly requires far more power than is necessary to increase its speed moderately slowly.

The economical driver always endeavours to make his car impart the sensation that it is rolling over the ground. Thus, instead of opening the throttle fully when it is required to pick up speed, the accelerator pedal should be depressed gently and gradually, the amount of depression increasing as the car picks up its speed, and decreased when the desired speed has been attained. This is what is known as driving on the high spot.

That Annoying " Flat Spot."

Most motorists are familiar with a flat spot—the position in the range of the accelerator pedal during which the engine shows no useful response to the increased throttle opening. This may be due to a variety of causes, although it is usually traceable to the means of compensation employed in the design of the carburetter, but it has a counterpart, viz., a high spot. The difference in the characteristics of the two is that, although normally there is only one flat spot in the position of the accelerator relative to one definite speed of the engine, a high spot can be found for all speeds. The discovery of a high spot does not take very much practice, for one can quickly tell by the feel of the engine when it is best accommodated by any particular throttle opening, the note of the exhaust helping in the ascertainment.

Economy by Using the Hand Throttle.

It is a very bad practice to keep varying the throttle opening, that is to say, to be continually altering the depression of the accelerator pedal, when a car is on the road. The continuous joggling of the throttle promulgates a surging action in the interior of the carburetter, which results in an imperfect mixture being obtained, and this naturally has a wasteful result. For this reason it is generally more economical (although less convenient) to drive on the hand throttle than it is to use the accelerator pedal. Especially does this apply on bumpy roads.

Fast hill-climbing, too, is another marked source of waste, and the economical driver always gradually increases the speed of his car as he approaches the foot of a short hill, so that the momentum is sufficient to assist him over the crest. This practice, it will be understood, is entirely different from that of rushing a hill by suddenly plunging down the accelerator in a frantic hope to get over the top without gear changing. Smooth, gradual acceleration and correct use of the gears when they are required are the proper methods to apply when economy is the aim.

CHAPTER XI.

Competition Driving. How to Make Racing Gear Changes. Preparing the Car for the Event.

Although competition driving has reached such a high pitch of development, there is certainly no need to regard those who persistently win gold medals in long-distance trials as anything after the nature of supermen. Generally they are very ordinary motorists, who have assimilated through experience a certain amount of knowledge, which, while it certainly gives them a distinct advantage over the ordinary amateur, has nothing in the nature of the mysterious or psychic in its make-up.

Very much the same applies to those who drive at Brooklands and in various speed events. One must give them credit for having nerve, the ability to do exactly the right thing at the right moment. Two chief personal factors which enter into competition in the motoring world are the ability to tune an engine and knack of rapid gear changing, and there is no reason why the average driver should not equal expert "performers" after a certain amount of practice. We are not speaking now of road racing, for that is a very highly specialized art of speed.

Local and Long-distance Events.

Those who read this book, however, will be more concerned with local hill-climbs in which their own cars are entered, or else long-distance reliability trials organized by the M.C.C., such as the London-Edinburgh, London-Exeter, London-Land's End, or shorter events. For speed work is must be realized that everything depends upon maintaining the revolutions of the engine. Given ideal conditions, the power unit should be running at the speed that represents its maximum power output from the moment the flag drops until the finishing line is crossed. Of course, this is impossible, but the nearer one gets to it the nearer and the more likely is one of putting up the best show of which the car is capable.

"Starting" Procedure.

Many inexperienced drivers lose a great deal of time at the start. The following is the proper procedure:— Normally, the starter counts "Five, four, three, two, one—Go!" and, as soon as he says "Five," the clutch should be put out, the first gear engaged, and the accelerator depressed until the engine is turning over steadily and fast. A revolution counter is a great help in competition. For instance, if the driver knows that his engine will do 3,500 r.p.m. in bottom gear, he should have his revolution counter showing that figure when waiting for the fall of the flag. Crack drivers even go so far as to let the clutch just rub slightly, even before the flag drops, keeping the car stationary with the hand brake. Then, instantly the words "One—Go!" are given, the hand brake goes off and the clutch comes in, the accelerator pedal goes full down—all simultaneously. The idea of allowing the clutch to rub slightly is to prevent too sudden a strain being thrown on the transmission.

To Change Up Quickly.

Now, between the starting line and finishing post in a hill-climb a skilful driver never dreams of lifting his foot off the accelerator. In order to change up quickly, therefore, a fierce clutch stop is essential, and it should be arranged so that it comes into operation at a point two-thirds way down the travel in the clutch pedal, so that when changing gear one simply stamps on the clutch pedal momentarily, at the same time swinging the gear lever through the gate, keeping the engine going full throttle all the time at a speed which it gathers during the period it is doing maximum revs., which period should not be longer than one second. It would be useful in imparting an added kick to the wheels when the clutch is let in again, the momentum of the flywheel adding useful speed to the car. Always remember when driving in a hill-climb to regard the finishing line as being at least 10 yards farther back than it actually is, so that there is no danger of cutting out or stopping the engine too soon. Much time can be saved by steering close into the hedge on corners ; in a hill-climb that is properly organized the road will be kept clear, so that you can make full use of the camber, swinging over to the right for a right-hand corner, and vice versa.

If a Skid Occurs.

If the car skids seriously, and if you must shut off for a moment in order to correct a skid, try to do it on the clutch, so that the engine speed is not reduced and its power output lessened. If a change down is essential, learn to change by slipping the clutch, and not double declutching, for it is much quicker ; that is to say, just ease the clutch pedal, still keeping the accelerator depressed, and make a fairly deliberate but very definite movement of the gear lever.

Attending to Details.

When tuning-up a car for competition it can generally be assumed that the carburetter will take a choke tube a size larger than that usually fitted. This, of course, only applies to speed events in which the rate of the engine revs. should be kept up. The thinnest oil possible should be used in the gearbox and back axle ; the wheels should be balanced by fitting equal weights opposite the tyre valves. The tyres should not be too hard, otherwise wheelspin will be prevalent, and if the event is to be decided on formula much good work could be done by examining the nature of the formula and discovering whether a higher marking will be obtained by ascending the hill slowly with a heavy load or fast with a light load. If the formula used by the club is one in which the time is squared, it usually pays to be light ; but when straight time is taken, then the car can be weighted up considerably. By bearing this in mind success can often be obtained where a failure would otherwise be almost excusable. For instance, if a car climbs a hill at a speed which is too fast for second gear to be used and too slow for third speed, then it must be weighted until second speed suits it to a nicety. By so doing a win on formula is fairly well assured, provided, of course, that the engine is in good condition.

Long-distance Trials.

Regarding long-distance road trials, there is very little indeed that calls for special ability, and, therefore, special instructions. It is important to read the regulations thoroughly at the start, and read them over and over again until you have memorized them and know more or less by instinct what you may and what you may not do on the day of the trial. A great deal depends upon keeping cool and not rushing. An average of 20 m.p.h. is not difficult to maintain so long as the car keeps going, but on no account should an unnecessary stop be made, for that only leads to undesirable speeding afterwards, and it is surprising how hard it is to make up time on a 20 m.p.h. average when the road is encumbered with other traffic, and especially if the stop has been made off the main road. One's mental outlook as well as physical condition counts enormously on a long-distance 24-hour event. Go to the start with your car really prepared down to the last detail. If you start tinkering around with your engine or chassis at the last moment, when at the perfectly natural excitement you will be keyed up to, it is ten chances to one that you will forget something or make some adjustment about which you are not quite sure, and that uncertainty will worry you for hours and hours on end in a most unpleasant fashion.

Freak Hills and "Nerves."

If there are any freak hills which are likely to have slimy surfaces included in the route, Parsons chains are practically essential. The quickest method is to carry the chains all ready fitted on a couple of spare wheels, changing the wheels themselves when the approach to the hill is encountered.

Nerves again play a very important part in freak hill-climbing. The great thing is to be in sympathy with your engine. Engines, like human beings, do not like being flurried, and there is no sense in rushing a hill, especially if it is a long one.

Duties of a Driver and Passenger.

On these long-distance trials it is essential that the driver and passenger should go to make up a perfect team, and each should have his duty allocated to him. For instance, at a check the driver should see about filling up the car with petrol, oil and water, while the passenger serves with the food or attendance. In exactly the same way, each should know what to do when a puncture occurs, so that the wheel is changed in a minimum of time, one operating the jack, while the other unscrews the spare wheel, etc. When the trial is timed to split seconds, it is, of course, advisable to practise driving dead to schedule. This can be done by saying that you will arrive under the clock at the local town at such-and-such a time, trying and trying again until you can do it. Incidentally, this is usually more a matter of driving slowly than fast.

CHAPTER XII.

Motoring Measurements, Calculations and Formulæ. Abbreviations in General Use.

In order to make specifications and descriptions more concise the following abbreviations are used: —

Millimetres = mm.
Centimetres = cm.
(Units of length).
Square centimetres = sq. cm. (Unit of area).
Cubic centimetres = c.c. (Unit of volume).
Revolutions per minute = r.p.m. (Rate of rotation).

Horse-power = h.p. (Power).
Brake - horse - power = b.h.p.
Pounds per square inch = lb. per sq. in. (Pressure).
Miles per hour = m.p.h.
Miles per gallon = m.p.g. (Fuel or oil consumption).

Bore and Stroke.

The bore and stroke are two important engine dimensions, usually stated in order to give an idea of the size of the power unit. These dimensions are generally expressed in millimetres. The bore is the internal diameter of the cylinder, this being practically the same as the outside diameter of the piston. The stroke is the distance traversed by the piston from its uppermost to its lowest position, during which time the crank makes half a revolution.

Cubic Capacity and Volume Swept.

The capacity of an engine (which is usually expressed in cubic centimetres) is the volume swept through or displaced by one piston during its stroke and multiplied by the number of pistons. It therefore depends upon the bore, stroke and number of cylinders. The calculation is made as follows:—First, determine the area of one piston crown in sq. cm. by squaring the bore (in mm.), multiplying the result by 22 and dividing by 2,800. Secondly, multiply this area by the stroke (in mm.), and divide by 10 in order to get the volume (in c.c.) swept by one piston. The capacity is simply this volume multiplied by the number of cylinders.

For example, take a four-cylinder engine with a bore of 70 mm. and a stroke of 120 mm. The area of one piston is 70 × 70 × 22 ÷ 2,800 = 38.5 sq. cm. The volume swept by one piston is therefore 38.5 × 120 ÷ 10 = 460 c.c. Hence the capacity is 460 × 4 = 1,840 c.c.

Engine Revs. and Car Speed.

The rate at which the engine revolves at any given car speed depends upon the gear ratio in use and the running or effective radius of the rear wheels as measured from the centre of the hub cap to the road. For calculations this radius may be taken as approximately equal to half the tyre diameter. First, determine the speed of the car in feet per minute by multiplying the speed in m.p.h. by 88. Secondly, determine the rate of revolution of the rear wheels as follows:—Multiply the speed in feet per minute by 42, divide the product by the tyre diameter (in inches) and divide the result by 11. Then the r.p.m. of the engine will be obtained by multiplying the rear-wheel r.p.m. by the gear ratio.

Example: For a car with 30-in. rear tyres and a gear ratio of 5 to 1, travelling at 20 m.p.h. the speed in feet per minute is 88 × 20 = 1,760. The corresponding rear-wheel r.p.m. is therefore obtained by the following steps:—(a) 1,760 × 42 = 73,920. (b) 73,920 ÷ 30 = 2,464. (c) 2,464 ÷ 11 = 224 rear-wheel r.p.m. Hence the engine speed is 224 × 5 = 1,120.

Gear Ratios.

The gear ratio can be defined as the ratio between the engine speed and the speed of the rear wheels ; it depends solely upon the gears employed between the two. On direct drive (top gear) the ratio is simply that which is determined by the back-axle gears; on indirect drives it is the top-gear ratio multiplied by the ratio provided by the gears in the gearbox.

The speed ratio produced by two meshing gears depends upon the number of teeth in each. A 15-toothed pinion driving a 45-toothed gearwheel gives a ratio of 3 to 1, the driven wheel revolving at one-third of the speed of the pinion, and so on. The top-gear ratio of the modern car is of the order of 5.0 to 1; bottom-gear ratio in the neighbourhood of 18 to 1. These figures express the number of times the engine crankshaft has to rotate for each complete revolution of the road wheels.

Speed and Distance.

If a car be timed over a measured mile the speed can be determined by dividing 3,600 by the time taken in seconds.

Example: If a car covers a mile in 90 seconds its speed is 3,600 ÷ 90 = 40 m.p.h. The following speed table gives the distance covered per second at various speeds:

10 m.p.h. = 14 ft. 8 ins.	60 m.p.h. = 88 ft. 0 ins.
20 m.p.h. = 29 ft. 4 ins.	70 m.p.h. = 102 ft. 8 ins.
30 m.p.h. = 44 ft. 0 ins.	80 m.p.h. = 117 ft. 4 ins.
40 m.p.h. = 58 ft. 8 ins.	90 m.p.h. = 132 ft. 0 ins.
50 m.p.h. = 73 ft. 4 ins.	100 m.p.h. = 146 ft. 8 ins.

Braking Distances.

Impossible claims are often made for the distances in which a car can be stopped. These distances vary with the square of the speed, so that for a car which can be stopped in 30 ft. at 20 m.p.h. the braking distance at 40 m.p.h. will be 120 ft., while at 60 m.p.h. 270 ft. will be required. At any given speed the most efficient of brakes cannot do more than just bring the four wheels to a point at which locking is imminent, so that the stopping distance is limited by the adhesion available between tyres and road. The following distances are those obtainable with a really efficient set of four-wheel brakes on a dry road; distances which are less than these at the speeds given are very seldom obtained:—

Speed (m.p.h.):

20	30	40	50	60	70	80

Distance (feet):

17	37½	66	105	150	213	266

To "stop the car in its own length," so glibly spoken of by motorists, is impossible unless the speed does not exceed 20 m.p.h., and even then this feat demands exceptional brakes and road adhesion.

Torque.

The torque produced by an engine is the turning effort which it can apply, and is usually measured in lb.-inches, as it involves both force and distance. Thus a force of 100 lb. applied at right-angles to a crank of 3-in. radius gives a torque of 300 lb.-ins. Engine torque can be calculated from the b.h.p. if the speed at which the power is developed is known; in most engines the torque is practically constant over a wide range of speeds.

Treasury Rating and Horse-power.

The rated horse-power of an engine for taxation purposes is obtained from a formula based upon the number of cylinders and their bore (internal diameter). The calculation is made as follows:—Square the bore (in millimetres), multiply by the number of cylinders and divide by the figure 1,613. Take, for example, a four-cylinder engine with a bore of 70 mm. The Treasury rating is $70 \times 70 \times 4 \div 1,613 = 12.1$ h.p.

Brake-horse-power.

Whereas the rated horse-power is an arbitrary figure, the brake-horse-power (b.h.p.) represents the power actually developed at the flywheel as determined by a brake test. It depends upon many factors, such as capacity, r.p.m., valve and port design, compression ratio and mechanical efficiency. Up to a certain limit the b.h.p. increases in proportion to the r.p.m.

HOW TO DRIVE A CAR.

The ordinary mechanical definition of a horse-power is a unit rate of performing work, viz., 33,000 foot-pounds per minute.

Compression Ratio and Pressure.

The compression ratio is defined as the volume of the space above the piston when at the bottom of its stroke, divided by the volume of the diminished space above the piston when at the top of its stroke ; ratios varying between 5 to 1 and 6½ to 1 are common. The compression pressure is that attained in the cylinder just before the spark fires the mixture, and for average engines is of the order 90 lb. per square inch.

Conversion Data.
(Approximates for Practical Purposes.)

To convert kilometres to miles, multiply by 5 and divide by 8.

To convert litres to pints, multiply by 88 and divide by 50.

There are 25.4 mm. in 1 in.

One kilogramme is equal to 2.2 lb.

One American gallon equals .83 of an imperial gallon.

One cubic inch equals 16.4 c.c.

One gallon of water weighs 10 lb.

One gallon of petrol weighs about 7⅔ lb.

A handy measure of an inch is a halfpenny.

A metre is 39¼ ins., against the 36 ins. of the English yard.

The freezing point on the centigrade thermometer scale is 0 degree and the boiling point 100 degrees. On the ordinary Fahrenheit scale, which is not much used for technical purposes, boiling point is 212 degrees and freezing point 32 degrees.

In one revolution a road wheel covers a distance equal approximately to 3 and 1-7th times its diameter.

CHAPTER XIII.

Motoring Legal Matters.

With the passing of the Road Traffic Act, 1930, the speed limit of 20 miles an hour became inoperative so far as motorcars and motorcycles are concerned. Increased penalties for dangerous driving are provided in the new Act and there is a new offence which is ''careless driving.''

Under the Act, too, every user must have a policy of insurance which will cover him against third-party risks, and he must have a certificate of insurance which must be produced on demand, or within five days at a police station named on a slip which a constable will provide. The same now applies to the driving licence.

The Driving Licence.

Five shillings is the cost of a driving licence, which is issued to any applicant, but a person under 17 years of age shall not drive a motor vehicle other than a motorcycle or an invalid carriage on a road.

Every applicant for a driving licence must make a declaration on the prescribed form as to whether he is suffering from any disease or physical disability which would be likely to cause the driving by him of a motor vehicle to be a source of danger to the public. A driving licence is obtained either by going to the County Hall, Westminster, if the applicant lives in London, or by applying for a form of application from the Clerk to the County Council of ———, County Offices ———, or, in the case of a County Borough, to the Town Clerk, Town Hall, ———. The forms should be filled up in every particular, and the 5s. fee enclosed, when a driving licence will be issued for one year from the date of issue. It should be signed on receipt.

HOW TO DRIVE A CAR.

Under the Act a publication known as the "Highway Code" is published, and all motorists should receive a copy with their first driving licence. Failure to observe any provision of the Code may in certain proceedings be relied upon by any party as tending to establish or to negative any liability which is in question. It is important, therefore, that every driver should keep his "Highway Code" for ready reference, as amongst other things it contains diagrams of the recognized hand signals, including those given by the police.

It is impossible to compress into a small space the new Regulations which have been issued under the Road Traffic Act. These have been excellently summarized by the Automobile Association and the Royal Automobile Club in handy pamphlet form, and members of those bodies are strongly advised to procure copies of them.

Registration.

Every car must be registered—that is, allocated an official number and index letters by which it is ever afterwards known. The numbers are displayed on plates at the front and at the back of the vehicle, but under the existing regulations it is permissible to paint the number on some part of the back of the car providing it is absolutely flat and vertical over its entire area. Letters, which must be white on a black ground, must be 3½ ins. high, and every part of every letter and figure must be ⅝ in. broad. A hyphen is not allowed between the letters and figures. The letters and figures are in one row on the oblong plate or the letters can be above the figures on the alternative design. A space of 1½ ins. must be allowed between the group of letters and the group of figures, but this space can be reduced to ¾ in. where the letters are placed over the figures.

A car licence is obtained from the same authorities as the driving licence, and when applying for it a form has to be filled in, giving various details, such as the chassis and engine numbers, colour of body, number of seats, etc.

HOW TO DRIVE A CAR.

Taxation.

The tax is on a basis of £1 per h.p. (or 15s. as from January 1, 1935), according to the R.A.C. rating, which is the same as what is termed the Treasury rating (see definitions and formulæ for method of calculation). Any part of a h.p. counts as 1 h.p. ; thus a car rated at 11.9 h.p. is liable to a tax of £12 per annum.

Quarterly licences are also issued at a slightly increased charge, and cars may also be licensed at any time up to the end of a year or quarter. An unexpired licence may be surrendered to the county council with whom the vehicle is registered, and a refund of the duty will be made in respect of each complete month of the period of the currency which is unexpired at the date of surrender.

Position of Licence.

When registering a car the owner receives a registration book containing particulars of the vehicle. This book need not be carried on the car, but must be produced by the owner at any time on request by a policeman, a Customs and Excise official or a local taxation official. A licence card is also provided, and this must be attached to, and carried on, the vehicle at all times when it is in use on the road. It should be in a holder adjacent to the windscreen facing towards the near side of the road and not less than 2 ft. 6 ins. from the ground level, between two parallel lines, the first drawn vertically through the rearmost part of the driving seat and the second drawn vertically 6 ins. in front of the base of the front-glass windscreen ; or, where no windscreen is fitted, a point 4 ft. forward of the first line.

Licences may also be carried facing forwards so as to be clearly visible from in front on the near (left) lower corner of the glass of the windscreen, or within 2 ins. of the glass, either in front or behind it, so as to be visible through the glass.

An annual licence may be taken out from January 1 to December 31 ; a quarterly licence dates from January 1 to March 24, March 25 to June 30, July 1 to

September 30, and October 1 to December 31. Part-yearly licences from any month to the end of the year are obtainable.

A licence should be examined from time to time. If the ink fades the owner is liable to be summoned and fined. A new licence will be issued free if it is proved that the ink has faded, but not if the holder is defective.

If the colour of a car is changed the licensing authority should be notified and the registration book and licence returned for the alteration to be made.

An owner must not himself make any alteration on any licence or registration book.

The fixing of a licence on the inside of the windscreen with gummed paper is contrary to regulations.

Car Changing Hands.

When a car changes hands both the seller and the purchaser must inform the licensing authority. The seller hands the registration book to the purchaser after writing the name and address of the new owner in the proper place.

If a licence or registration book has been lost the licensing authority will issue a duplicate on payment of 5s.

A rebate of 25 per cent. is allowed off the tax of cars the engine of which can be proved to have been made before January 1, 1913.

A tax has not to be paid on a car not in use.

There is no tax rebate for professional and medical men.

Lighting.

Two front lights must be carried by all two-track motor vehicles.

One rear red light compulsory for all motor vehicles, including motorcycles.

Parked vehicles may be exempted from showing lights in certain specified parking places.

A vehicle towing another vehicle need not show a red light, unless distance between vehicles exceeds 5 ft.

A light showing to the front need not be displayed by a vehicle whilst it is being towed.

Dipping headlights and combined dipping and swivelling headlights legalized, and headlights that move in conformity with the front wheels when they are turned for the purpose of steering are permitted, subject to certain conditions.

The lamps must be kept in efficient condition and show light visible from a reasonable distance.

No vehicle may show a red light to the front, or any light other than a red light to the rear.

These regulations do not extend to Ireland.

Under the powers given by the Road Vehicle Lighting Act additional regulations may be made from time to time on various matters connected with the lighting of vehicles. They will be reported fully in *The Motor*.

During Summer Time the lighting-up time is between one hour after sunset and one hour before sunrise. For the remainder of the year between half an hour after sunset and half an hour before sunrise.

Reporting an Accident.

If a motorist is concerned directly or indirectly in any accident on the highway, it is his duty to stop and, if required, to give his name and address. If he is unable to give his name and address, he must report the accident at a police station or to a police constable as soon as reasonably practicable, and in any case within 24 hours of the occurrence. The term "animal" means any horse, cattle, ass, mule, sheep, pig, goat or dog.

Minor Offences.

All cars must be fitted with efficient silencers, and cut-outs whereby a free or open exhaust may be provided at will are forbidden.

Identification marks, number plates, etc., must always be easily visible, and must therefore be kept free from mud and dust ; neither may they be obscured by overhanging luggage, rugs, etc.

Motorcars must be equipped with either (a) two entirely independent and efficient braking systems, or (b) one efficient braking system having two independent means of operation.

If the car is left standing unattended the engine must always be stopped.

Except in such places as are recognized parking grounds, a car must never be left at the roadside for any appreciable time, as action is liable to be taken for obstruction. In many thoroughfares three minutes is considered sufficient by the authorities.

A motorcar must not be left on a road in such a position as will cause it to be a danger to other traffic or vehicles.

A motorcar must not travel backwards for a greater distance or time than may be requisite for the safety or convenience of the occupants of the vehicle and of the passenger and other traffic on the highway.

Traffic Regulations.

In certain large towns a one-way traffic system is in use. There will always be found warning notices.

White lines are often painted at corners to define clearly the two halves of the road. Motorists should always be careful to keep on the proper side of such lines, which, incidentally, serve to remind drivers of the danger of attempting to pass another vehicle on a corner or hill.

Automatic Traffic Signals.

In a number of towns there are automatic signals at crossings for controlling traffic. These consist of coloured lights which change at regular intervals. Particulars as to towns so equipped can be had from the Automobile Association.